inspired by nature: Minerals

THE BUILDING / GEOLOGY CONNECTION

Alejandro Bahamón

Patricia Pérez

W.W. Norton & Company
New York • London

For information about permission to reproduce
selections from this book, write to Permissions,
W. W. Norton & Company, Inc., 500 Fifth Avenue, New York, NY 10110

For information about special discounts for bulk purchases, please contact
W. W. Norton Special Sales at specialsales@wwnorton.com or 800-233-4830

Library of Congress Cataloging-in-Publication Data

Bahamón, Alejandro.
[Arquitectura Mineral. English]
Inspired by nature : minerals : the building/geology
connection / Alejandro Bahamón, Patricia Pérez.
p. cm.
Includes index.
ISBN 978-0-393-73260-3 (pbk.)
1. Architecture—Environmental aspects. 2. Minerals—Social aspects.
3. Nature (Aesthetics) I. Pérez, Patricia. II. Title.
NA2542.35.B32 2008
720'.47—dc22

                                                    2007045567

W. W. Norton & Company, Inc.,
500 Fifth Avenue, New York, N.Y. 10110
www.wwnorton.com

W. W. Norton & Company Ltd.
Castle House, 75/76 Wells Street, London W1T 3QT

0 9 8 7 6 5 4 3 2 1

Introduction
Patricia Pérez

The act of "petrifying" in architecture—far removed from the evil designs of a monstrous Medusa who petrified her enemies with her stare to kill them—has been and continues to be an attempt to make a building project endure, to perpetuate it or immortalize it, from both the tectonic and metaphorical viewpoint.

petrify. (from Latin petra, stone, and facere, make)
1. Transform or turn into stone, or harden something to make it seem like stone.
2. fig. Leave one immobile with astonishment or terror.

From the Paleolithic Period (from the Greek, *paleos* = old and *lithos* = stone)—the time in prehistory when human beings understood that there was no better refuge from the dangers that beset them than a cave, the interior of a rock—until today, mineral materials, particularly stone, have played a key role in the design and construction of buildings. Although stone has admittedly been superseded by concrete and steel as a structural element, it still serves an essential function as cladding and decoration.

However, the persistent use of stone throughout the history of architecture cannot be explained solely on the basis of its physical characteristics. The panoply of minerals, which range from small crystals to large masses on the surface of the earth, has been linked—and is so now, at least in part—to mythological or religious beliefs about the origin and evolution of the planet.

The history of architecture is dotted with highly symbolic stone monuments that are capable of transcending themselves: prehistoric menhirs used in worshiping the gods, Egyptian obelisks that conveyed the stability and creative power of the god Ra, and the pyramids, which not only represented the sun's rays that would allow the dead Pharaoh to rise to heaven but also symbolized the primordial mound from which Ra created the world. These are just some of the many examples that could be mentioned in this context.

lay the first stone. fig. Perform the ceremony of placing the foundation stone in a building due to be constructed.

Nowadays, "petrified" architecture, in the most metaphorical sense of the term, uses stone to expresses feelings of hardness, stability, impenetrability, resistance, and perpetuity—what better hiding place for a treasure than that rock which opened up on the command of "Open, sesame"?—or it takes advantage of the formal language of precious stones as a vehicle for conveying sensations associated with jewelry, such as elegance, transparency, luxury, power, perfection, wealth, etc.

Beyond any semiotic interpretation of the term "petrified architecture," however, any architecture that turns to the mineral world also embraces the interpretation, translation, and appropriation of geological forms on different scales, as well as the processes that intervene in their appearance, transformation, and destruction. Various approximations of the nature of minerals—from models of the symmetrical organization of crystals and their forms of growth to the creation and molding of the earth's relief—can serve, from a practical viewpoint, as a support for the solution of structural and/or design problems and help a building adapt more effectively to its environment, or act as a model by providing architectural units with growth patterns on different scales.

This book gathers together the work of several architects who have looked for answers in the world of minerals. This selection of architectural projects, conceived on the basis of interpretations of minerals, is complemented by reflections that encourage us to investigate new approaches to architecture inspired by geology.

In parallel to these, we offer, among others, a study of crystallization, which serves as a reference for the increasing number of architects who refuse to recognize fixed limits, and a study of structures that erode and accumulate, echoing the geomorphologic processes that give shape to the earth's relief. It is important that observation of the mineral landscape can provide a key to understanding the forces of nature that hold sway over a specific place, as well as a vehicle for the solution of problems derived from the complexity of a building's adaptation to its setting. As for subtractive architecture, this appears as a representation of the act of emptying, as a process for creating spaces in negative, in contrast to the conventional approach, characterized by the addition of material.

We have also considered it appropriate to include a chapter devoted to volcanoes, in order to reveal architecture's powerlessness against the virulence of certain geological phenomena. We also present examples of architecture in volcanic areas that incorporate symbolic allusions to these phenomena.

As a final reflection and a means to discuss monolithic architecture intent on simplicity of form, we refer to a book by the Viennese architect Adolf Loos that establishes a link between crime and ornament. Loos, with his idea of reducing decoration to the utmost, stated that the tomb, as a piece of architecture, must be a "modern" object with no "tattoos," such as the cube, the classical symbol of the earthly—and he took this concept to its limits in the project for his own grave. His words stand as the "last stone."

"I want my tomb to be a granite cube—but not too small, as that would make it look like an inkwell." **A. Loos**

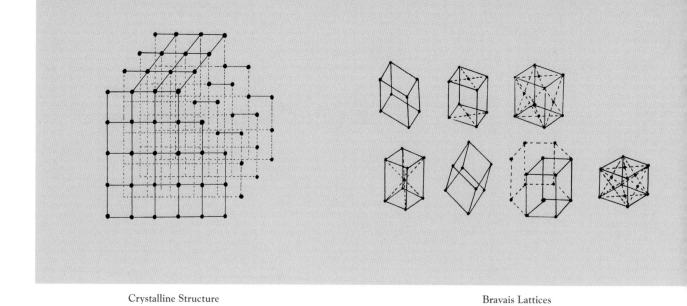

Crystalline Structure   Bravais Lattices

Crystals

Ever since the time of Ancient Greece, the need to find a method for rational and explicit design has led human beings to turn to nature. In the history of architecture, the search for formal solutions that could stand as models of perfect equilibrium, harmony, and proportion has mainly focused on the organic realms of plants and animals. Since the discovery of X-rays, however, the inorganic and mineral spheres, with their systems of geometrical proportion, have not gone unnoticed.

Crystals, the epitome of a classic ideal of beauty, are minerals with structures defined by their flat faces and a form that reflects the inner order of their atoms. The basic unit (known as the unit cell)—made up of a specific, fixed number of atoms of a certain type—is repeated in all three directions of space to form a crystal lattice, which is distinguished by its symmetry. There are 14 types of crystal lattices, each defined by 14 types of unit cells. When the 14 lattices and the position of the atoms in the unit cell are combined and repeated in accordance with a specific symmetry, there are 230 possibilities of distribution (called space groups). The classification of these space groups according to their symmetrical elements gives us 32 classes of symmetry which, in turn, are grouped into seven crystalline systems: cubic, tetragonal, hexagonal, rhombohedral, orthorhombic, monoclinic, and triclinic. All

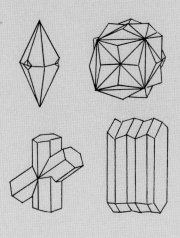

| Crystal Systems | Crystalline Aggregate |

these regular models of symmetrical organization found in crystalline forms can become suitable models for architectural design—models that serve as an inspiration for the geometrical organization of a building's elements and volumes, the topological interrelationships between rooms, the structure of the circulation, etc.

Apart from the fascination of crystals' symmetrical forms, their regular growth process is of equal interest to architecture. A logical, geometric mesh similar to a crystal lattice, which regulates and coordinates the formation or growth of a body in space and time, is undoubtedly of great interest in projects that seek formal definition on the basis of a growth process: both a crystal and an architectural work can attain a complex but orderly structure through an incremental growth based on a minimum unit complemented by a further series of units. This process of self-formation or crystallization can mediate between architecture and nature, in order to legitimate a construction that aspires to be natural, without any need to draw on idioms proper to the organic world. Architectural projects conceived from a logical, geometric mesh that regulates and coordinates a unit's formation or growth can lead to constructions with dynamic, open surfaces with no fixed limits, capable of responding to unexpected external influences.

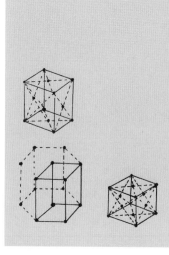

Bravais Lattices

In the context of the small group of synesthetic artists who have treated visual art and music as inextricably linked elements, Carsten Nicolai continues to take his creative process in new directions. Originally trained as a landscape architect, Nicolai found his first means of expression in painting before establishing a unique style on the borders between art, science, and sound. In his search for connections between visual and acoustic perception, he has created a far-reaching body of experimental work that aims to break down the barriers between our different sensorial experiences and transforms natural scientific phenomena like sound and light frequencies into occurrences that can be perceived by the eyes and ears. Syn Chron is Nicolai's most ambitious project to date in its attempt to create a symbiosis between architecture, light, and sound. The work, designed as a traveling installation, was mounted for the first time in the main lobby of the Neue Nationalgalerie in Berlin. Conceived as a mobile space that serves as an acoustic body, a resonance space, and a projection surface all in one, it comprises a crystalline architectural volume with a translucent cladding that acts as a vehicle for acoustic and optical interventions. Electronic music, composed by the artist himself, creates a modular rhythm that is reflected in the laser projections. The composition, which remains in operation day and night, is also intended to be a support for live performances.

Flattened View of the Structure

Client
Galerie EIGEN + ART Leipzig/Berlin

Type of Project
Artistic installation

Location
Traveling installation

Total Surface Area
1,076 square feet (100 m^2)

Completion Date
2005

Photos ©
Christian Gahl, Uwe Walter

Traveling Installation

Syn Chron

Carsten Nicolai

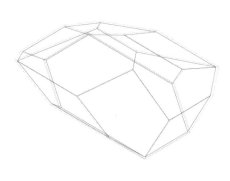

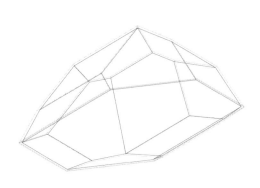

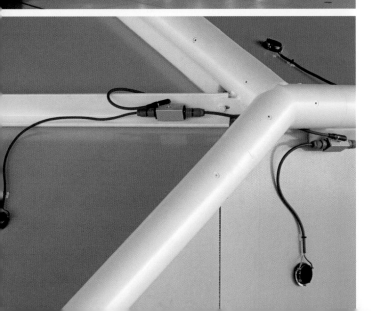

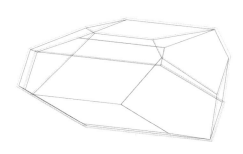

Digital Models

This architectural installation is a space with light and sound that visitors can observe from inside or outside, or even from a distance. The basic structure consists of a tubular steel frame that echoes the geometric forms typical of crystals. This made it possible to create a stiff, free-standing piece clad with very light translucent panels. The module had to be easy to dismount, as well as being able to withstand adverse weather conditions so that it could be set up outdoors. This prototype of mobile architecture was developed in conjunction with the architects Finn Geipel and Giulia Andi and the engineer Werner Sobek. The sound is carried via small transmitters on the outside of the panels, while the images on the polygonal panels come from four projectors inside.

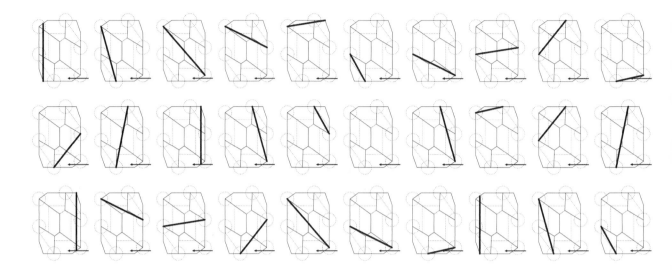

Diagrams Showing the Configuration of the Movement of Laser Projections and Sound.

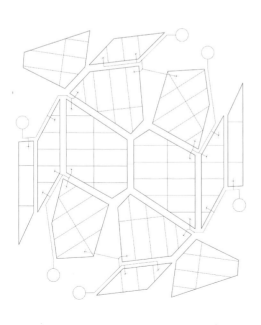

Flattened View of the Assembly

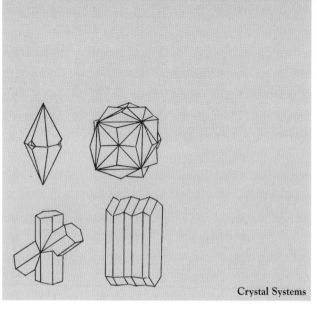

Crystal Systems

The design of this cinema complex in a central neighborhood in Dresden had to first take into consideration the urban impact of a building of this scope. According to the architects responsible for the project, public space in European cities is sharply deteriorating as a result of a lack of government funds, and this situation triggers the sale of urban land to private property developers intent on making the maximum profit from single-function buildings with little or no relationship with their surroundings. This project does away with the idea of a single function by incorporating urban activities into the building itself, with the aim of generating a new type of city planning. This approach not only advocates the inclusion of public space inside a building but also this space's interaction with other key areas in the city. The interrelationship with other squares, public interiors, and walkways sets up a dynamic sequence, defined by tangents and diagonals rather than orthogonal axes. The UFA complex, formulated as the connection between Pragerplatz and St. Petersburger Strasse, has become a public space in its own right. The project is defined by two closely interconnected volumes: the concrete block containing the eight movie theaters and the glass shell that serves as both lobby and public square.

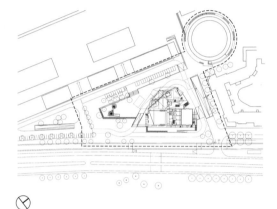

Site Plan

Client
UFA Theater AG

Type of Project
Cinema complex

Location
Dresden, Germany

Total surface area
66,456 square feet (6,174 m²)

Completion Date
1998

Photos ©
Gerald Zugmann

UFA Cinema Complex

Coop Himmelb(l)au

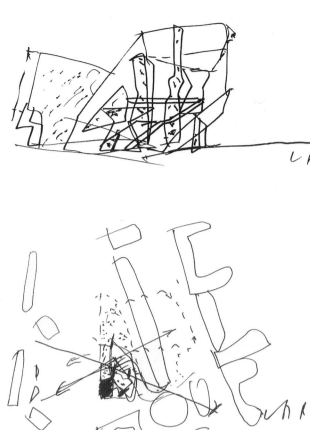

Preliminary Sketches

The glass shell is visually striking when seen from outside and represents more than just a lobby for circulation on the inside. It is an urban walkway, with bridges, ramps, and staircases that lead to the various theaters and reveal the to-and-fro of people, both inside and outside the building, as well as on the different levels. The public space is thereby split into three dimensions, creating a lively atmosphere that evokes the dynamism of a film. The Skybar, a tensioned steel structure in the form of two cones, is a bar—open to the general public—that floats in the middle of the main lobby.

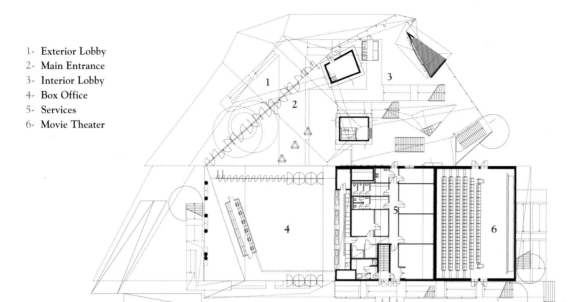

1- Exterior Lobby
2- Main Entrance
3- Interior Lobby
4- Box Office
5- Services
6- Movie Theater

Ground Floor

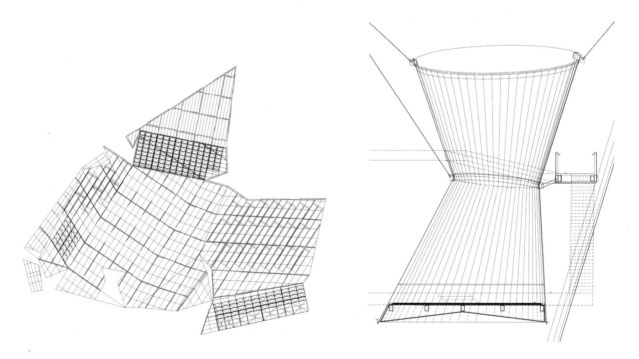

Flattened View of Glass Structure

Structure of the Floating Bar

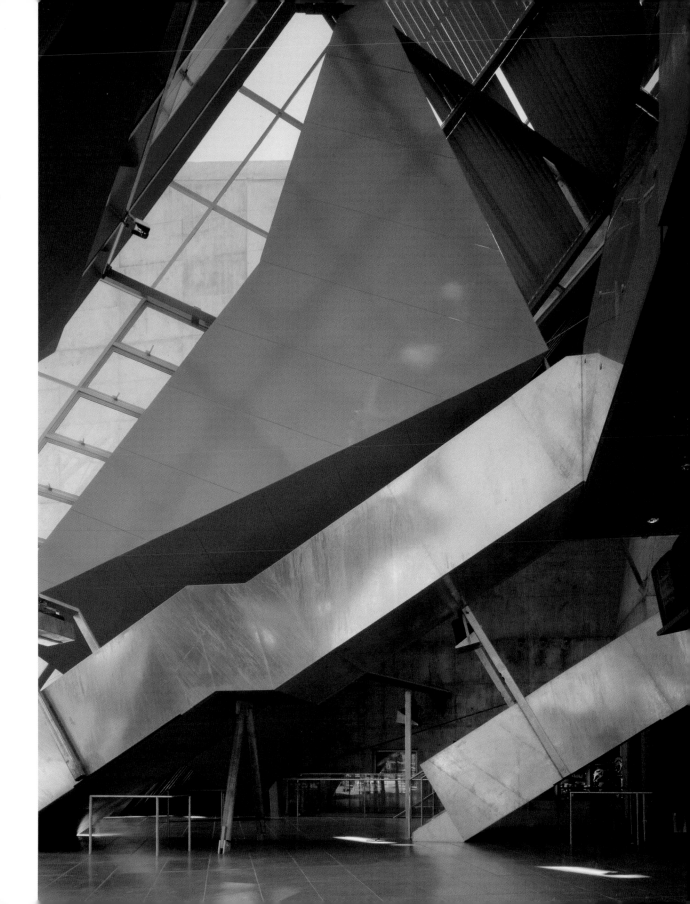

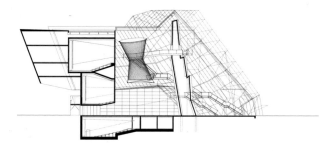

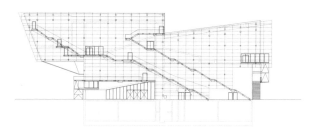

Cross Section

Longitudinal Section

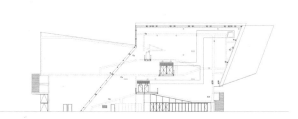

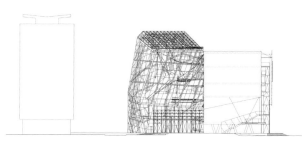

Elevations

The concept of the crystal-building makes the contents of the building visible from the city, just as the city itself is visible from inside the building. The concrete block with the movie theaters is permeable at street level, with views of the traffic on the busy streets surrounding the complex. The staircases and ramps that provide access to the theaters all originate in the glass space, while the administrative areas are set on the least busy sides of the building. All the design strategies try to generate an interior-exterior building that maintains a permanent dialogue with the city. The interior activity is projected outward to enhance the creation of this new urban space.

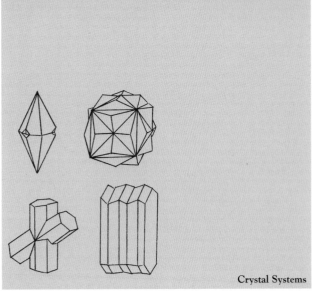

Crystal Systems

As we have seen in the introduction to this chapter, a crystal is defined in chemical and mineralogical terms as a solid body made up of atoms, molecules, and ions grouped in a strict, regular order to create a pattern that extends in three dimensions. This building for the Glad Tidings Community, a small Christian group in the midst of a predominantly Muslim area, is intended as a new place of worship for community use in London's planned Olympic neighborhood. The intervention proposes the demolition of an old chapel and the construction of a multipurpose center. In this respect, the building's crystalline form is a reflection of its internal processes, in terms not only of the structure and interior design, but also of the hoped-for relationships to be set up between the building, its users, and the neighborhood in general. Crystals are formed when molecules are subjected to a process of solidification. Under ideal conditions, the result can be one simple crystal, with all the atoms compressed inside the same crystalline structure. Many crystals, however, are formed along with others during solidification, resulting in a polycrystalline solid. This building represents the consolidation process of the Christian community itself and its urban expression as a distinctive presence within the neighborhood. The members of the Glad Tidings Community from the area refer to the building as their "shining crystal."

Ground Plan

Client
Glad Tidings Community

Type of Project
Community facility

Location
London, England

Total Surface Area
4,521 square feet (420 m^2)

Completion Date
2007

Images ©
Mueller Kneer Associates

London, England

The Crystal (Unbuilt)

Mueller Kneer Associates

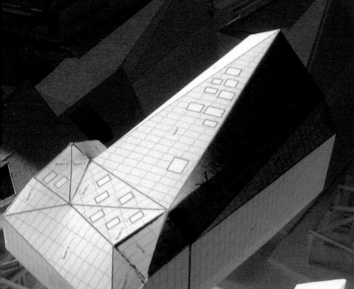

Model of the Volume

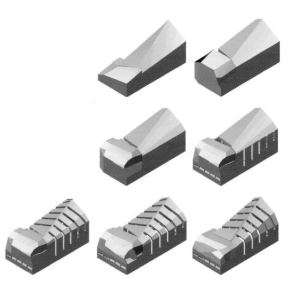

Sections and Elevations with Respect to
Neighboring Buildings

In order to evaluate the visual impact that a building of these characteristics can create in such a dense urban context, various studies of shadows were undertaken in order to establish the appropriate volume for the building. Several scale models were combined with digital images to find the form most suited to the setting. The idea was to produce an object that was visually striking but didn't overwhelm the adjoining properties, which are traditional two-story brick buildings, typical of the East End of London. These parameters determined the geometry of the cladding for the building, whose final crystalline form is the result of the solidification of the various studies of shadows.

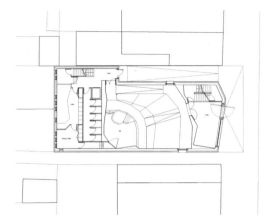

Site Plan

Ground Plan

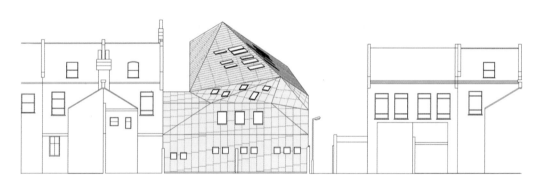

Front Elevation

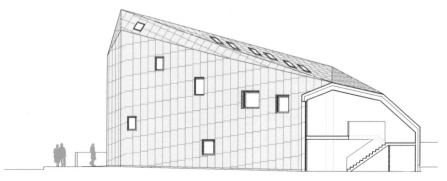

Cross Section

The Crystal, as the project has been christened by the architects themselves, contains a hall for religious services, as well as other auxiliary spaces set within the same iconic form. A copper alloy has been chosen to make the large sheets that serve as cladding, which changes appearance once it is in place and exposed to air and water. Over time, the climatic conditions will gradually transform the material's characteristic golden-red colors and endow it with striking color combinations. Each façade will develop its own personality. The interior is open-plan, with various areas interrelated and benefitting from the spatial qualities derived from the building's form.

Crystalline Aggregate

This project consists of a small extension to a building dating from 1750 that was originally built as a chapel and later turned into a family house. It is set on a steep, rugged slope, a few hundred yards above a dense wood. The client's main requirement was a modern, functional home that retained the solid, mystical character of the original construction. This demanded an approach that established links with the design language of the old structure while also bearing witness to the arrival of a new era. None of the building's dialectical elements should be predominant, so it was decided to place the new piece slightly apart from the old one, in symmetry with its original L shape, to create a new T-shaped composition. The formal solution for the new volume comprises a cube resting on a pedestal on the edge of a rock, a bright-red crystal in the middle of the wood: a ruby. Its color acts as both a contrast to and a mediator between the existing structure and the surrounding wood. The strategy of creating a "jewel house" emerges as an innovative solution that refers to the natural setting while emphasizing the solidity and mysticism of the old building.

Site Plan

Client
Andrea Siebenhofer

Type of Project
Family house

Location
Steyr, Austria

Total Surface Area
646 square feet (60 m²)

Completion Date
1997

Photos ©
Paul Ott, Hertl.Architekten

The Ruby

Hertl.Architekten

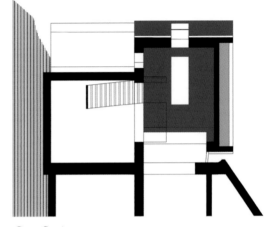

Cross Section

The new volume is situated to the rear of the house, in such a way that it is only visible from the lower part of the valley. The red color and the effect of depth were obtained by painting the brick and by applying a second skin made up of industrial glass panels. Both these devices make the ruby gleam from a distance, although its structure, color, and sheen can be perceived very differently depending on the climate, the season of the year, the time of day, and the position of the observer. Only a thin, horizontal crack interrupts the solidity of the volume to allow the inhabitants to enjoy a panoramic view of the valley. Inside the ruby, the atmosphere is mainly dark and subdued, apart from the horizontal slash framing the landscape.

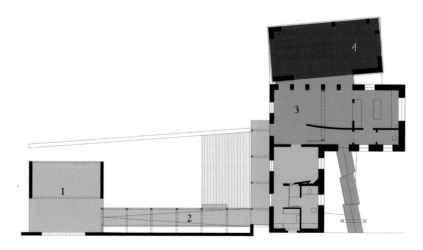

Ground Plan

1- Parking Lot
2- Ramp-Arcade
3- Old House
4- New Extension

The enigmatic exterior of this extension is achieved by using a double façade to cover the volume, while also providing heat insulation for the interior space.

Crystalline Aggregate

The Diamond House is an office and studio space designed as an annex to a preexisting house, set in a deep canyon opposite a steep, rocky slope, with difficult access and little terrain suitable for construction. Direct sunlight reaches the lot for only a few hours a day, and the lay of the land made it necessary to build deep retaining walls to create robust foundations for the new structure. After analyzing these extreme determining factors, the architects came up with a design strategy based on two basic premises. First, the development of a geometric form that would adapt to the base provided by the terrain, as well as the mountainous landscape, the preexisting house, and the requirements of the foundations. Second, the need to find a material and construction system independent of the solid structure that would be light and porous, as well as capable of reflecting the limited sunshine and adapting to various forms and conditions. The structure's geometry, based on that of a diamond, allowed it to adjust to the existing architecture while also establishing a dialogue with the rugged landscape. After considering various options based on patterns in the natural surroundings, the architects chose a symmetrical sequence resembling a filigree of thin cords in the form of a diamond. After several tests, stainless steel and the diamond shape emerged as the most appropriate combination for maximizing the reflection of sunlight and guiding it inside the space.

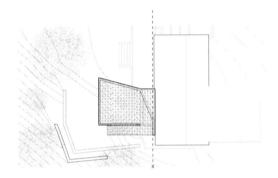

Plan of the Roofs

Client
Private

Type of Project
Annex to a house

Location
Santa Monica, California

Total Surface Area
646 square feet (60 m²)

Completion Date
2008

Images ©
XTEN Architecture

Santa Monica, California

Diamond House

XTEN Architecture

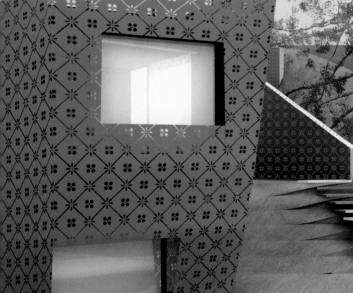

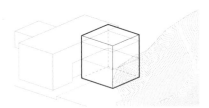

Initial State of the Lot

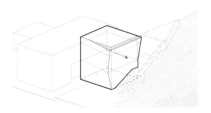

Deformation Made by the Program

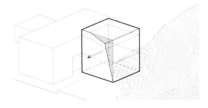

Deformation of the Terrace

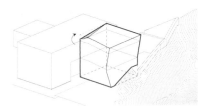

Fold Over the Existing Volume

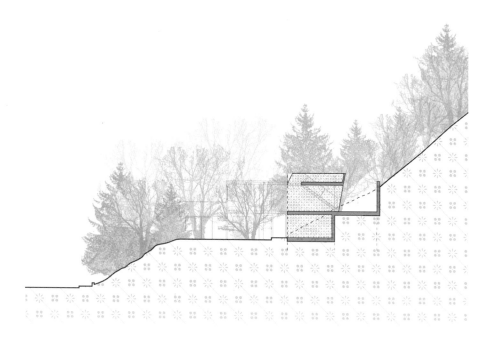

Longitudinal Section

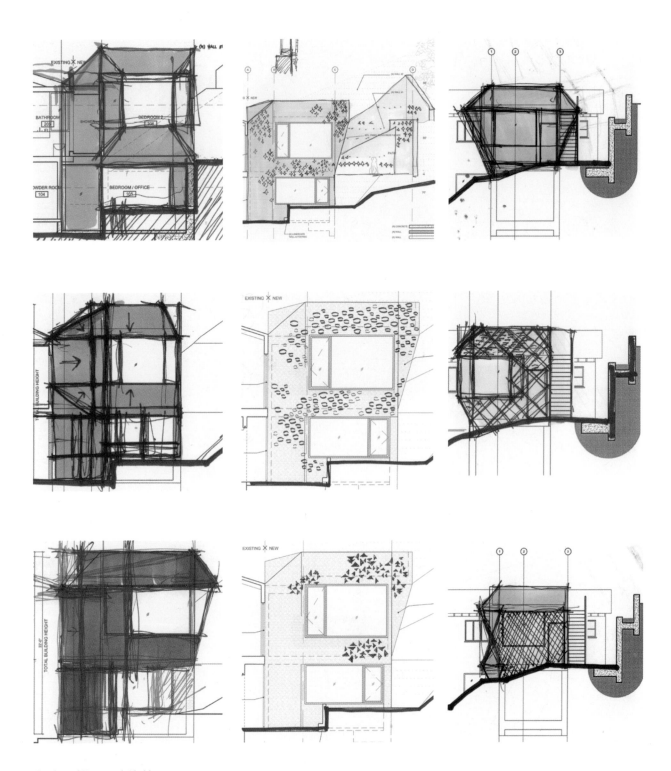

Studies of Form and Cladding

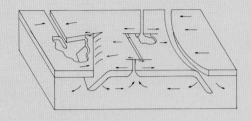

Movement of Tectonic Plates   Granite Landscape

The Earth's Relief

Apart from processes involving the earth's internal activity, or tectonic activity that causes some areas to create relief by rising or falling, there are other external processes that level the earth's surface by removing or accumulating sediments, often with a time span observable by the human eye. The morphology of the huge structures generated by the earth's internal powers—mountains, hills, and other forms of relief—are gradually destroyed by the action of climatic agents and the force of gravity itself. This molding of mineral forms gives rise to most of the mineral landscapes we see.

The main agent intervening in the molding of terrestrial forms is erosion. This is a process which, through the action of water, ice, or wind, leads to the fragmentation of rocks, producing materials that are transported to other regions. Through a process of lithification (petrifaction), this fragmented material produces sedimentary rock. It is difficult to imagine an architecture based on erosion, an architecture which, under the influence of the action of external agents, would be worn away until it disappears. However, as a concept for temporary or ephemeral structures, an erosionable construction could fall under the category of sustainable architecture, because the elimination of its own ruins would be incorporated into the project itself. Equally curious would be the case of an architecture that built itself by intercepting and accumulating material, a dune architecture, a structure that would collect sediments and create its own carcass by shrouding itself in them.

| Fissure | Karst Landscape |

Furthermore, the interpretation of the molding of a mineral landscape can be the key to understanding the forces acting in a particular place. The reading of the signs of mineral forms can become a valuable source of information for the solution of architectural problems derived from the complexity of a building's adaptation to its climatic conditions. Obviously, a rock's behavior in the face of the action of water, wind, or the force of gravity depends on its composition. Stone is made up of minerals with varying degrees of resistance, depending on its hardness, the geometrical distribution of its particles in crystalline material, its tensile strength or resistance to breaking, its specific weight, etc. These differences in composition can give rise to mineral topographies as different from each other as a karst landscape and a

granite one. While the former is made up of soluble carbonated forms, with a morphology characterized by the presence of small-scale reliefs and subterranean cavities, the latter is notable for the disintegration of rocks into balls or rounded forms.

The relationship with a local context marked by the presence of harsh geological forms can suggest the form or the tectonic character of an architectural project. Without any need for a building to turn into a total architectural materialization of the terrain, as if it were just yet another topographical sinuosity, the mere appropriation of basic textures or forms from the mineral environment can often be a way of improving a building's integration.

Karst Landscape

This project involved the extension and renovation of the Denver Art Museum, originally designed by the Italian architect Gio Ponti in 1972. The new project was mainly intended to house the museum's new collections of contemporary art, as well as exhibits focusing on architecture, design, and Oceanic art. The building also had to incorporate a new main entrance for the entire complex, a lobby reflecting the scale of the new project, and access to stores, a cafeteria, and a theater. The general composition of the building's volumes was primarily inspired by the vitality of Denver, a booming city in the American West set at the foothills of the imposing Rocky Mountains. This mountain range was formed by compression in a roughly east-west direction that caused the earth's crust to rise some 65 million years ago. The volumetric proposal for the museum's extension was based on a reinterpretation of the abrupt, angular geometry that defines the Rockies' landscape. The use of materials emphasizes both the building's echoing of the landscape and its most innovative features. The native stone covering the plazas and some of the blocks in the composition reinforce the integration with the urban environment around it, while the titanium sheets cladding most of the façades give it an avant-garde, hi-tech look.

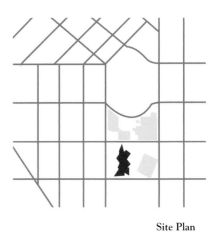

Site Plan

Client
City of Denver, Denver Art Museum

Type of Project
Cultural facility

Location
Denver, Colorado

Total Surface Area
145,313 square feet (13,500 m²)

Completion Date
2006

Photos ©
Bitter Bredt

Denver, Colorado

Denver Art Museum

Daniel Libeskind

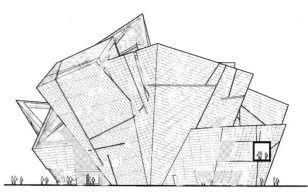

North Elevation

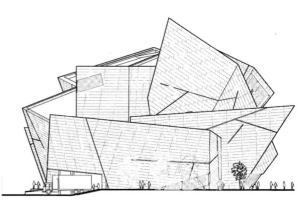

South Elevation

One of the project's major challenges consisted in responding to the extraordinarily wide range of transformations in the city's light, coloring, atmospheric effects, temperature, and climatic conditions. This integration had to be not only physical and functional but also cultural and experiential. The new building was designed to be an architectural icon that contrasts with its traditional surroundings; it was not conceived as an isolated building but as part of a composition of public spaces, monuments, and avenues. The floor plan responds to all these physical and social variables, which exert a pressure on the composition comparable to that of the geological forces that gave form to the nearby mountain range. The project's spatial spectrum defines a choreography of public spaces that makes a greater impact on visitors than the construction in itself.

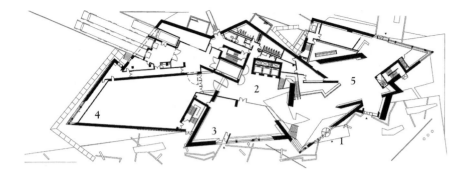

Ground Floor

1- Main Entrance
2- Lobby
3- Shop
4- Temporary Exhibitions
5- Permanent Exhibitions
6- Offices

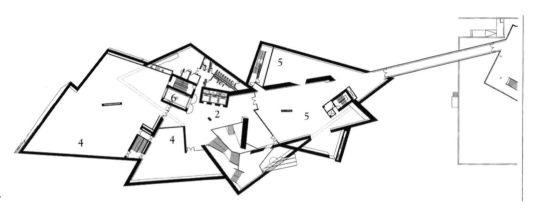

Second Floor

Third Floor

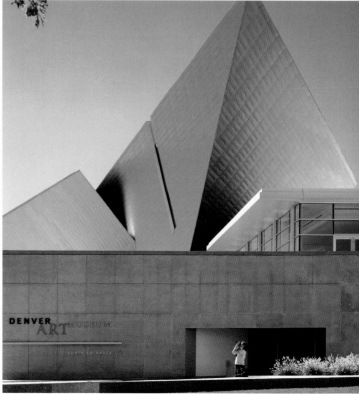

The formal interpretation of the Rocky Mountains—resulting in fragmented, angular volumes—and the use of titanium as a cladding material combine to create an object that stands out strongly in its urban setting.

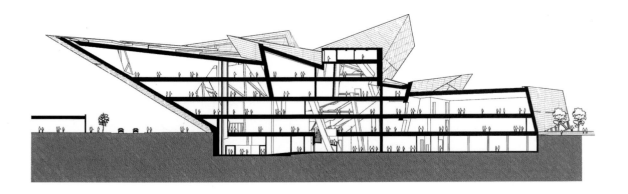

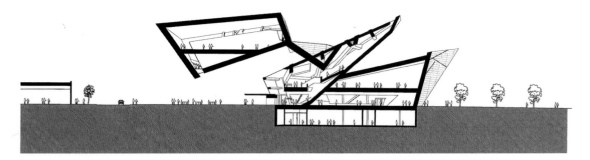

Longitudinal Sections

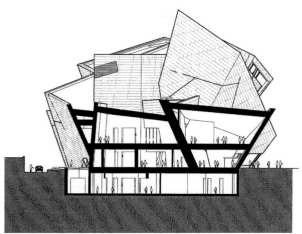 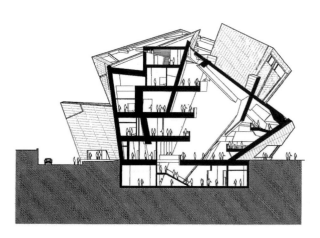

Cross Sections

According to the building's architect, its design follows the twenty-first century's trends in the creation of museums. The old barriers between tradition and avant-garde proposals are dissolved and reformulated in a new architectural program. The project tackles ecological issues and the role of architecture as an agent integrating with the environment. The light and the systems incorporated into the building interact with the visitor. The museum is no longer a form of abstraction but rather a place that reflects the desires of the public, and it therefore uses the latest technologies and fuses them with tradition to create a harmonious whole.

Fissure

The Spencer Theater for the Performing Arts represents the culmination of a quest shared by both architect and client to converge architecture, landscape, and the scenic arts. The building on the Fort Stanton plateau in New Mexico lies between two mountains that dominate the landscape with their imposing presence: the Sunset, to the east, and the Sierra Blanca to the west. This mountain setting marks the course of the sun in the summer months, and it constituted the first reference in the decisions about the building's exterior form and operation. The project was conceived as a white mountain, an enormous mass of solid stone, sculpted to set up the appropriate relationships with the light, the panoramic views, and the required activities. The intense annual program of touring theater shows unfurls in a volume with an analog image of the nearby mountains. The composition is based on a trapezoidal form, as seen by the gradual opening up in an east-west direction toward the stage area. On the south side, which receives the most sunlight during the day, the administrative offices, halls, and café are arranged around a central courtyard that is totally isolated from the exterior landscape.

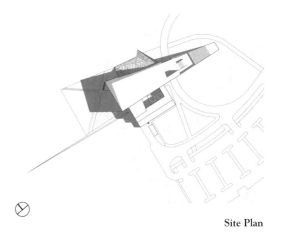

Site Plan

Client
Jackie Spencer, Spencer Foundation

Type of Project
Cultural facility

Location
Alto, New Mexico

Total surface area
52,097 square feet (4,840 m²)

Completion Date
1997

Photos ©
Tim Hursley

Spencer Theater for the Performing Arts

Antoine Predock

The bulky appearance of the general composition—which resembles a geological formation on the most rugged side of the plateau—presents a fissure in the northern end, from which a crystalline figure appears to emerge. Like a large lantern embedded in the landscape, this crystal volume—a translucent shell made up of a series of triangular panels of laminate glass in various sizes—marks the entrance from the exterior and serves an interior distribution space. This striking double-height volume, which hosts large meetings in the center, sets up a contrast to highlight the closed, massive volume. Various fissures in that architectural mass create the connections between the different areas, and between the entire complex and the exterior space.

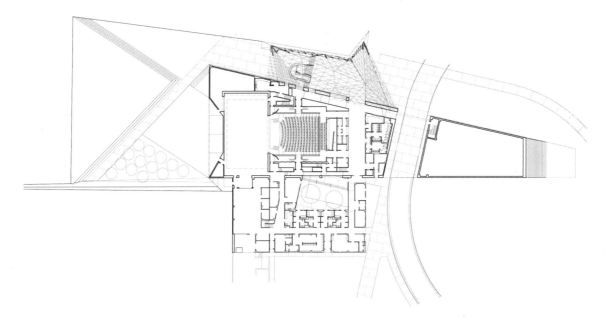

General Plan

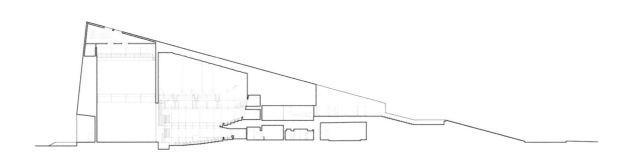

Longitudinal Section

The project proposes a progressive circulation: a vertical component is reached from a horizontal one inside the building. A soft light emanating from the crystalline element attracts the visitor from a distance and creates a panoply of geometrical interplays that are projected onto the theater's smooth surface of solid stone. Once inside, the crystal also marks the ascent to the upper levels, which culminate in a VIP room on the top floor. From this exceptional viewpoint, the plateau is rediscovered and the two chains of mountains framing this natural landscape can be fully appreciated. The complex, with its intense artistic schedule, has consolidated its position as a regional nerve center, now integrated into the Fort Stanton plateau.

Granite Landscape

The construction regulations of Tokyo's metropolitan government stipulate that the city's residential buildings must have spaces exclusively reserved for parking bicycles and for garbage collection. Normally, this part of a program usually occupies an insignificant place, literally subordinate to the rest of the volume. However, the most striking aspect of this apartment building in Tomigaya, a residential neighborhood in Tokyo, is precisely the small cabin that serves the twin functions of parking for bikes and collecting garbage. The architect joined the two together, as both need to be somewhere easily accessible from both inside and outside the building, and he placed this small architectural element on the northwest corner, the most visible part of the lot, with a visual opening of 70 degrees, at the junction between the small road and the broad avenue that define the lot on two of its sides. Just as if it were a chapel, a sacred site with an exterior form reflecting a deep enigma, this volume does not correspond to any theory or preconceived formula in particular but rather to the architect's own impulse. In fact, he is still unable to identify the compositional origin of this portion of the project. What is beyond doubt is that it reflects a response to very deep impulses and that its exterior cladding of metal sheets changes its appearance over time—two characteristics shared by the relief formations on the earth's surface.

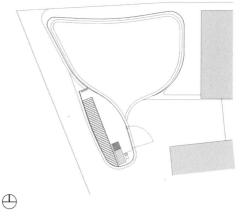

Site Plan

Client
Keiichi Umehara

Type of Project
Residential amenity

Location
Tokyo, Japan

Total Surface Area
538 square feet (50 m²)

Completion Date
2005

Photos ©
Koichi Torimura / Nacása & Partners

Tokyo, Japan

Tomigaya Apartment Building/Cabin

Satoshi Okada Architects

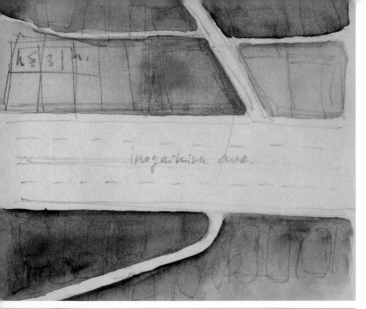

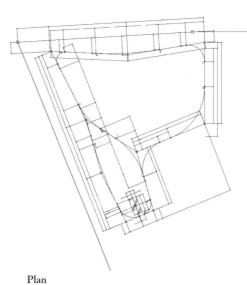

Plan

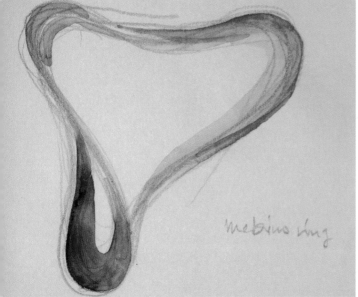

mebius ring

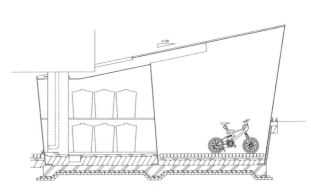

Cross Section

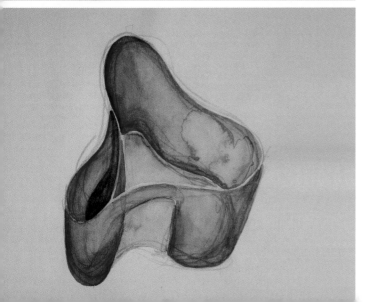

At the start of the design process, the architect sketched various images on paper and then created several models with light, flexible cardboard. These models allowed him to speculate on the idea of creating an architectural object on the basis of a single continuous strip that would give rise to a space divided into two parts: one for bikes and another for garbage. After investigating different possibilities, he came up with a balanced, albeit still tentative, composition, which he digitized to establish its dimensions and create a viable construction. This small element, considered as a fragment of a landscape rescued from another world, has grown into a visual statement that distinguishes this residential building from the many others around it.

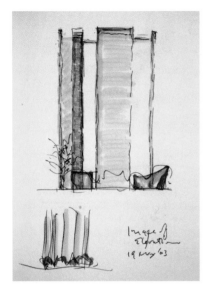

Preliminary Sketches

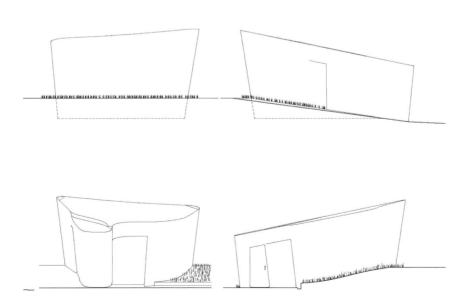

Elevations

The steel surround, exposed to the effect of rusting as if it were an ephemeral installation alluding to the erosion of the earth's surface, generates an evocative visual impact in the midst of the residential neighborhood around it.

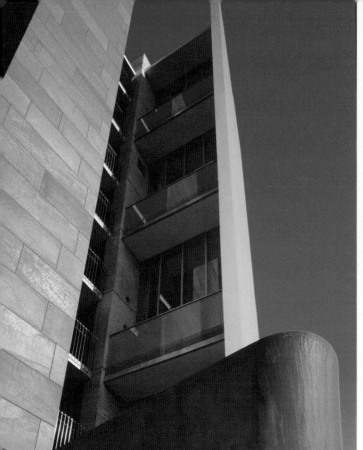
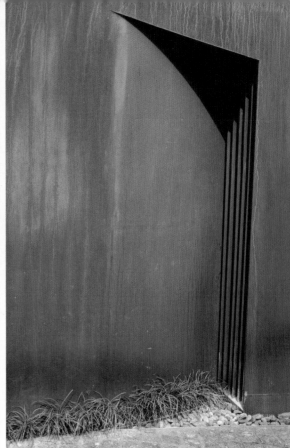

The sinuous movement of the steel strip makes it possible to create the interior division required by the program, as well as subtle openings that provide an entrance and windows in the form of thin fissures.

Karst Landscape

This residence's sculptural appearance, which creates an immediate visual impression, reflects the architect's intention to produce a metaphorical composition suggesting a canyon. A series of walls emerging from the ground like the geological formations typical of the Arizona desert around the house establishes a sequence of spaces running from the main entrance to the more private rooms. These walls, which grow in an asymmetrical fashion, draw the eye toward the angular geometry governing the layout of the building, while also highlighting the striking desert landscape all around. The general composition, based on the forms of that very setting, also makes it possible to appropriate outdoor space through a series of patios and terraces in which architecture becomes convergent with the horizon. The basic housing needs are developed on two levels, grouped toward the natural slope, in the northeast part of the property. The ground floor, half-embedded in the rock, opens up onto the southwest side of the lot to take full advantage of the natural light. The upper story, set in parallel with a sequence of rocks, responds to the brusque lay of the land and accommodates the maximum number of windows opening to the outside.

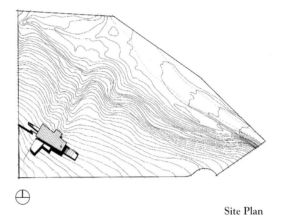

Site Plan

Clients
Bill and Carol Byrne

Type of Project
Family house

Location
Scottsdale, Arizona

Total Surface Area
4,306 square feet (400 m²)

Completion Date
1998

Photos ©
Bill Timmerman

Scottsdale, Arizona

Byrne Residence

Will Bruder Architects

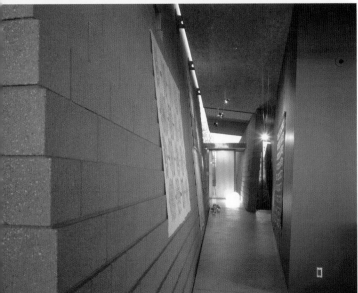

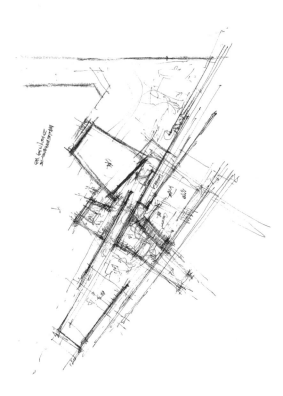

Preliminary Sketch

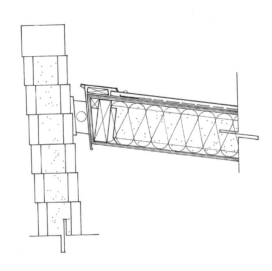

Construction Detail

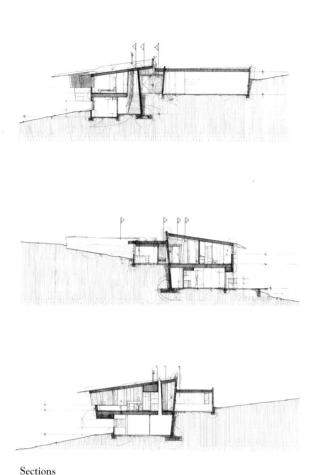

Sections

The vertical tilt of the building's load-bearing walls dramatically frames the panoramic views of the landscape. The walls' reinforced-concrete structure provides traction by means of curved metal supports linking them at the top. The project's mimetic qualities are emphasized by the use of materials and finishings typical of the region, such as sand, gravel, and the aggregates derived from the lot itself, as well as the rustic finish of the exterior walls. In the phases prior to the excavation for the building's foundations, the materials available for the construction and the outer cladding were carefully examined and selected, resulting in an effect that made the leaning walls seem like folds in the land itself.

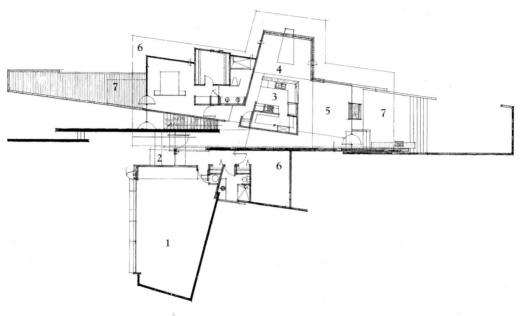

Second floor

1- Parking Lots
2- Entrance
3- Kitchen
4- Dining Room
5- Living Room
6- Bedroom
7- Terrace

Ground Floor

8- Studio
9- Bedroom

As a complement to the concrete walls, and as a contrasting element in the project's general composition, a series of components, interior walls and ceilings, were installed with plaster, copper, or galvanized steel. These materials, with their palette of colors ranging from purple to pale brown, are intermixed to create an interplay, with a mixture of textures, always based on the landscape outdoors. In fact, their appearance would change with the passing of time, and their perception varies according to the time of day, the weather, and the season of the year. Finally, the general enclosure was constructed with nonreflecting glass, made to measure to adjust every window and door to the building's formal language.

Fissure

The original commission involved the creation of a new sports campus for the Ewha University of Seoul, South Korea. The project had to resolve not only the needs of the building, but also the complexities of the terrain and its relationship with the campus as a whole and the district of Shinchon, to the south. The intervention demanded a response that went far beyond the lot itself, on an urban scale, and entered into the realms of landscaping, with the intention of mingling the urban fabric with that of the university. The creation of an artificial valley incorporating a sports belt introduces a new topography that affects the surrounding landscape in various ways and fulfills several functions at the same time: it provides a new entrance into the university's general campus, a place for everyday sporting activities, a field for annual festivals, and, above all, a point of connection between the city and the university. The sports belt, reminiscent of a horizontal fence, shows the life of the university to the inhabitants of Shinchon, and vice versa. Inside this artificial valley, the to-and-fro of pedestrians takes on a positive visibility, thereby creating a new public space that is buzzing all year round. This cleft excavated in the topography makes it possible to establish links in an east-west direction between different buildings on the campus that were hitherto completely unconnected.

Site Plan

Client
Ewha Women's University

Type of Project
Cultural facility

Location
Seoul, South Korea

Total Surface Area
753,474 square feet (70,000 m^2)

Completion Date
2007

Images ©
Dominique Perrault

Campus of Ewha Women's University

Dominique Perrault

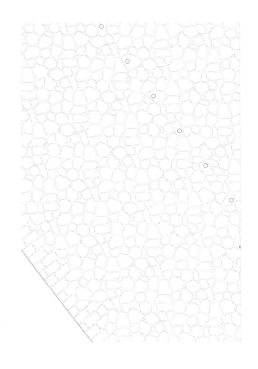

Details of the Stone Paving

Although the university is now totally absorbed into Seoul's metropolitan area, the campus's most outstanding feature is surely its natural elements. The building's exterior appearance, based on the movements of the topography, reflects the desire to highlight this characteristic. The lawn, flowers and trees constitute the building's cladding, completely subordinating its architecture to the general landscaping concept. The natural stone used to create staircases and esplanades furthers this process and helps to achieve an idyllic garden, ideal for special meetings, informal open-air classes, or pure and simple relaxation. This use of materials emphasizes yet again the interconnection between the project, the campus, and the city by diluting the barriers between old and new, between building and landscape.

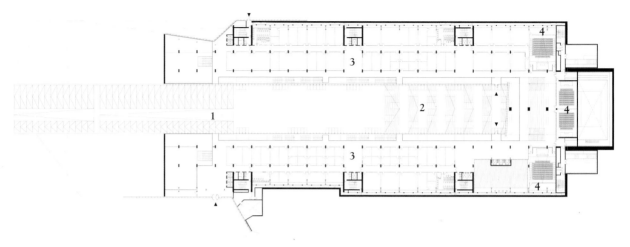

Ground Floor

1- Entrance Ramp
2- Bleachers
3- Classroom Area
4- Meeting Rooms

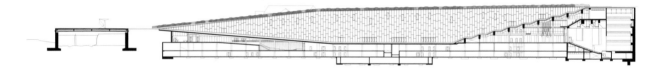

Longitudinal Section

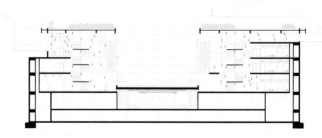

Cross Section

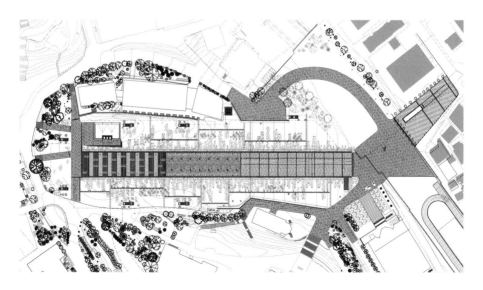

General Ground Plan

The artificial topography provided by this project gently leads the visitor from the exterior to the lobbies and classrooms inside, on a path leading through a series of multipurpose spaces.

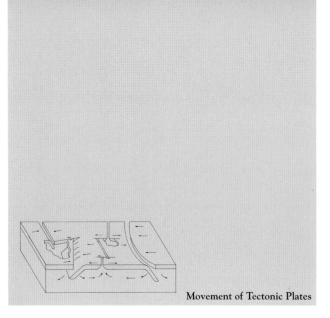

Movement of Tectonic Plates

Odile Decq is one of the few female architects with an international reputation. Along with her partner, the late Benoît Cornette, Decq won the Golden Lion in the 1996 Venice Biennale, whose theme was "architecture as a seismograph of society." Her architecture displays a predilection for high technology, but it is primarily characterized by a concept of permanent tension between interior and exterior, between volumes and space. Ducq won a competition for proposals for the new museum for the Liaunig Collection in Neuhaus, a small town in southern Austria. Herbert Liaunig is the owner of one of the country's biggest art collections, comprising almost 2,000 works by Austria's leading artists, from Herbert Boeckl to Fritz Wotruba. Liaunig invited five architects to submit ideas for the museum, and this project came out on top on account of its respectful understanding of its surroundings. Odile Decq describes the building, which is set on natural hills, as a "museum as a form of landscape" and defines it as "a concept that plays with the landscape." The project took its cue from the gentle folds and slopes of the terrain, reinterpreting them in the form of mobile, wavy roofs based on hyperbolic glass parabolas that seem to fly over the building. The interaction between the land and the building defines a visitor's path through the museum.

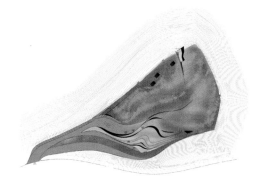

Site Plan

Client
Herbert Liaunig

Type of Project
Museum

Location
Neuhaus, Austria

Total Surface Area
48,438 square feet (4,500 m²)

Completion Date
2007

Images ©
Odile Decq Benoît Cornette

L Museum

Odile Decq Benoît Cornette Architectes

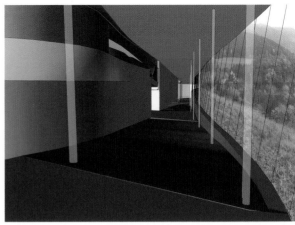

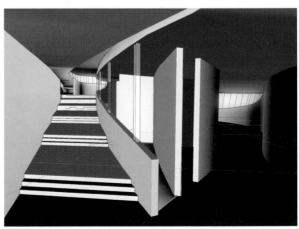

Interior Views of the Museum

The building's architectural language is based on the form of the roofs, which seem to emerge from the ground itself, echoing the hills surrounding the building. These large surfaces have been warped, twisted, and compressed to create an innovative observation point overlooking the valley, the town, and the castle. The waves on the roof stretch beyond the building and serve to give shape to the paths leading to it, as well as some outdoor terraces, thus increasing the perception of a "museum as a form of landscape." The entrance leads to the museum's various galleries through a glass corridor enclosed by a sloping curve that emphasizes new views of the surrounding landscape, creating a sense of adventure marked by a series of discoveries. Each space evokes continuous movement and tangential views, while offering varying viewpoints of the artworks inside and the landscape outside.

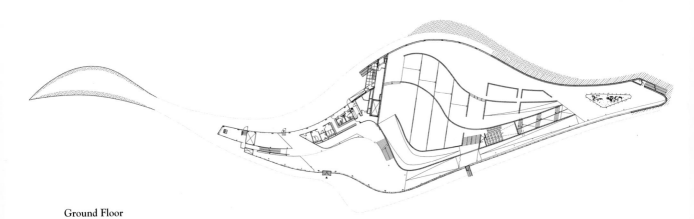

Ground Floor

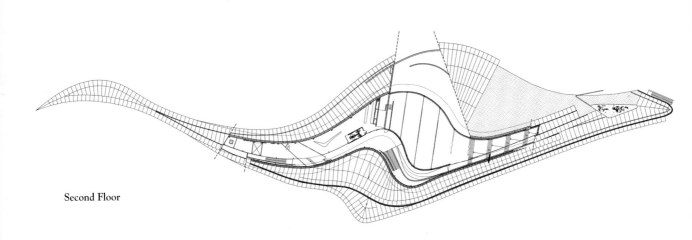

Second Floor

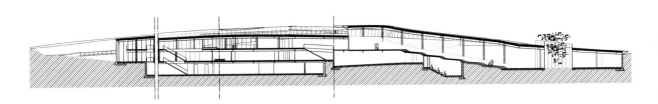

Longitudinal Section

The topography around the project has been modified by means of wavy strips of garden, which reiterate the forms of the roofs and so help integrate the building even more fully into the landscape.

Cave Section   Calcite Cave

Mineral Voids

Caves, chasms, geodes, and other forms of cavities are different expressions of a single reality: the absence of mineral material within a mineral body or form. There is no more expressive embodiment of what are commonly known as voids, hollows, or holes than those found in the vast world of minerals. The origin of these voids can vary. In the case of holes in limestone, water is the culprit, as it dilutes the material and drags it away. In volcanic areas, caves can be the result of cavities trapped between outpourings of lava, while rocks of all kinds can obviously create caves by detaching themselves from a mass. Extractive activities can also give rise to caves, albeit artificial ones: quarries are opened up to mine minerals, rocks are excavated to create platforms or terrain adapted to new uses, tunnels are bored

to make way for roads, and caves can even be dug out for residential purposes.

Subtractive architecture receives its name from the action that generates it. Unlike conventional architecture, which is built through the addition of material, in this case a form is created through the absence of material. One of the main advantages of this "negative" process is its capacity to create naturally load-bearing architecture, by exploiting the power and cohesion of the land or rock that gives it its form. This type of construction—which mankind has used for centuries, especially in rural settings, as shelter for livestock, as storage for tools, and as homes—has acquired a renewed importance in the quest for sustainable, environ-

<table>
<tr><td>Chasm</td><td>View from the Interior</td></tr>
</table>

mentally friendly construction. Caves' ability to maintain balanced temperatures in both winter and summer—due to the earth's capacity for storing heat and providing insulation—make cave homes outstanding examples of bioclimatic architecture. Their subterranean settings, or the fact that they are wrapped in mineral material, mean that they exist without being seen and so integrate effortlessly into the landscape.

There is another noteworthy characteristic of the act of digging into a rock for architectural purposes: the possibility of bringing to light mineral structures. Over and above the potential esthetic virtues of bare rock and the embellishment it can bestow on a project, architecture can be a vehicle for exposing layers or strata featuring fossils or other evidence of a site's geological history. Architecture that starts from a void to create habitable space and makes manifest the geological archive hidden in the mineral form to integrate it into its project can be termed "palimpsest architecture," directing our gaze toward the mineral world.

Finally, with respect to the enrichment of an architectural project by the discovery of rock outlines, we should mention the increasingly common example of spaces that have previously been emptied for other purposes, as in the case of quarries. Places that are rendered obsolete once material has been extracted from them can be turned into dramatic settings for new buildings.

Chasm

Tadao Ando, thanks to his approach to the interpretation of traditional Japanese culture and the modern world, is undoubtedly one of the most significant exponents of contemporary architecture. With no formal academic training, he opened his own architecture studio in Osaka, Japan, in 1969. His projects reject the consumerist materialism of today's society—so evident in other new Japanese architecture—but do not spurn contemporary materials and techniques. In his quest to create spaces that evoke positive sensations, he has managed to create his own architectural language, distinguished by the simplicity of its forms, the meticulous handling of light, and the presence of water. The Chichu Art Museum was built on Naoshima, a little island linked administratively to Shikoku, the smallest and least populated of the four islands that make up the Japanese archipelago. It is a place with which Ando has been closely connected since 1988, as he has developed three projects there. The lot for the Chichu Art Museum is situated on the crest of a hill, which still displays traces of an old marine lake. The design strategy was the same as the one Ando applied years before to the Benesse House and its annex (some 1,969 feet [600 m] to the east), where he buried part of the building, to the benefit of the natural landscape around the project. In the more recent project, Ando went even further and buried the entire museum in order to preserve the beautiful setting of the Seto Inland Sea and the hill.

Site Plan

Client
Naoshima Fukutake Art Museum Foundation

Type of Project
Museum

Location
Naoshima, Japan

Total Surface Area
29,633 square feet (2,753 m²)

Completion Date
2004

Photos ©
Tadao Ando, Mitsuo Matsuoka

Naoshima, Japan

Chichu Art Museum

Tadao Ando Architect & Associates

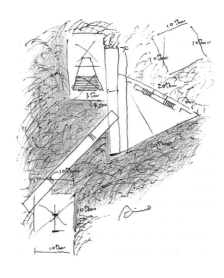

Topography of the Roof

Tadao Ando

Façade Details

The museum contains a permanent collection featuring three artists: the Impressionist Claude Monet and the contemporary artists Walter De María and James Turrell. Like the rest of Ando's work, this project is notable for its geometric rigor, spatial purity, and, above all, the masterful control of light. The desire for drama was satisfied by emptying the mountain and the composition of the three main spaces that make up the project. The main exhibition wing and the entrance wing are endowed with, respectively, a triangular courtyard and a square one, both completely sunken into the land, while the exterior corridor acts as a trench connecting the two areas.

The elegant, unbroken fissure running across two façades in one of the inner courtyards constitutes an extremely subtle structural and constructional device. It provides an unsupported light over 131 feet (40 m) long that accompanies visitors on their path inside the building.

Second Level Down

1- Entrance and Shop
2- Office
3- Stairwell
4- Lobby
5- Machine Room
6- Management Office

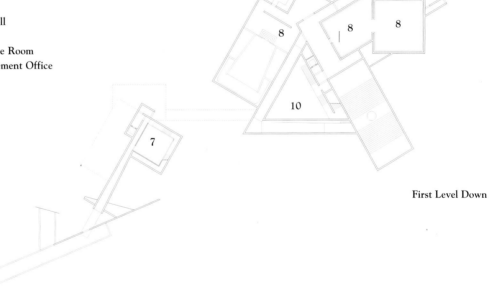

First Level Down

7- Entrance Courtyard
8- Galleries
9- Café
10- Courtyard

Ground Floor

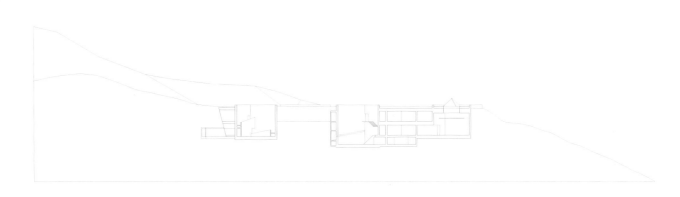

Longitudinal Section

Despite being totally buried, this building offers visitors a constant connection with the exterior and panoramic views of the coast. The contours of the hollows in the land emerge on the surface, thereby linking the crest of the hill with the interior of the museum. The geometrical figures created by these hollows are the only elements organizing the composition, although they do not reflect any pre-conceived directionality. Furthermore, the natural slope of the land enables the areas around the edge of the hill to allow completely unimpeded views. The galleries were developed in close collaboration with the modern artists involved and the director of the museum.

View from the Interior

Zonzamas is situated within the municipal area of Teguise, in the center of the island of Lanzarote in the Canary Isles, between the towns of San Bartolomé and Tahiche. This plain is famous for its archeological site, with the islands' highest concentration of remains of their ancient inhabitants. After decades of bureaucratic measures, it has now been possible to develop an architectural project devoted to the study and display of the culture of the island's primitive population. Apart from objects found in the excavations, reproductions of the local settlements will also be exhibited. Every element's position and its relationship to the physical environment was therefore vitally important, as the views, incidence of sunshine, dominant winds, crops, and topography all had to be scrupulously assessed and respected. The main design strategy consisted of sinking the large mass of the museum into the land, underneath the crop fields. The surface is broken by cracks that allow light to penetrate inside the galleries. On the east and west sides, where the volume is completely buried, lighting and natural ventilation are attained by means of tubes that emerge at the surface. The fact that the building consists of an artificial cave immediately summons up images of archeological digs and the rudimentary shelter of the island's first inhabitants—and these echoes are reinforced by the rough, basic form of the building's windows.

Aerial Photography

Client
Patrimonio Histórico de Canarias, Cabildo Insular de Lanzarote

Type of Project
Cultural facility

Location
Lanzarote, Spain

Total surface area
48,395 square feet (4,496 m²)

Completion Date
2007

Photos ©
AMP Arquitectos, Hisao Suzuki

Zonzamas Archeological Museum

AMP Arquitectos

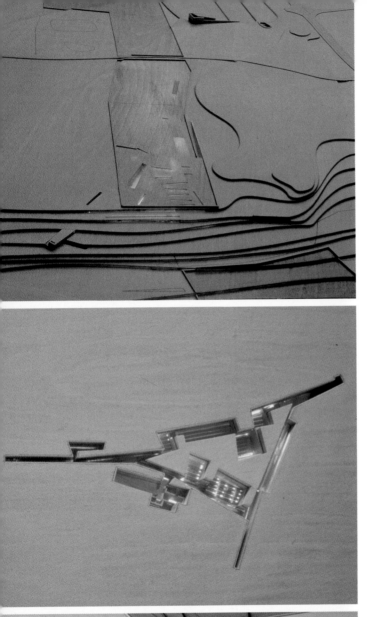

Preliminary Sketches

The museum is reached via the road that crosses the plateau from Arrecife, the island's capital, and ends in a large esplanade by the entrance. This large square is endowed with an almost imperceptible slope of 3.2%, which guides automobiles and buses 10 feet (3 m) below ground level. This subtle device succeeds in minimizing the presence of motor vehicles in such a flat and fragile landscape. The parking lot is set on the east and west sides of the volume, while the northern side houses the ticket office, entrance, and start of the museum tour, which unfurls in a succession of spaces excavated from the land to explain various aspects of the Canary Islands' earliest inhabitants.

The museum's main volume can only be seen from the excavated area (6 feet [5 m] below the natural ground level), where an exterior exhibition space has been installed in the form of an inner patio.

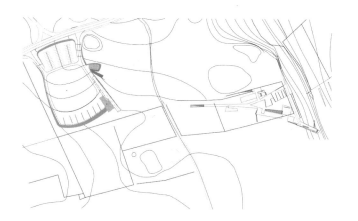

General Ground Plan

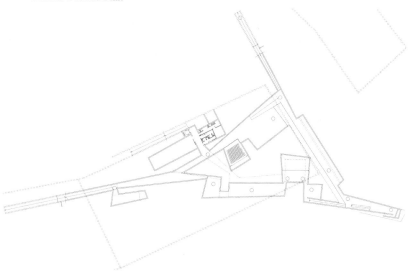

Ground Floor

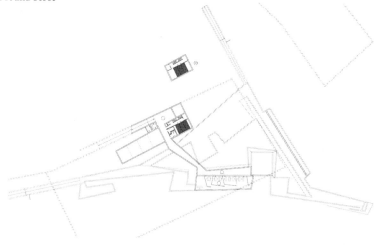

Second Floor

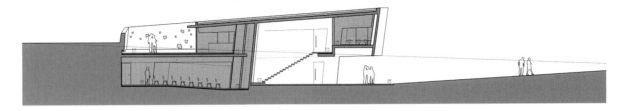

Longitudinal Section

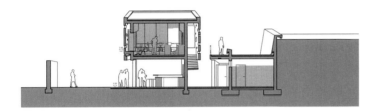

Cross Section

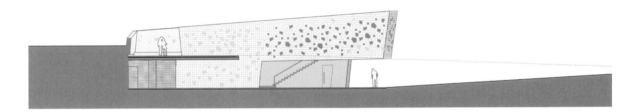

Side Elevation

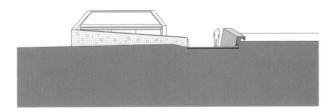

Front Elevation

The long ramp leading to the building's main entrance, which has been excavated from the rock, makes the outdoor landscape itself the first stop on the path through the museum. Inside the building, darkness reigns, to re-create the sensation of being inside a primitive dwelling. Light is very carefully introduced, through thin cracks or rough openings, to bring out the depth of each setting. The exhibition galleries have been conceived as spaces that are sufficiently flexible to host a collection that is still in the process of being unearthed. The option of a structure that bears loads by means of curved reinforced-concrete supports makes it possible to have a technical department in addition to the galleries, so that installations can be received or modified in accordance with the demands of each exhibition.

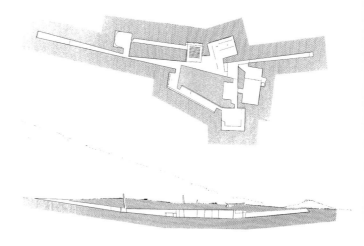

Plan and General Cross Section

Calcite Cave

The Netherlands' program for the construction of embassies and consulates in developing countries has earned them a reputation for promoting architecture that responds creatively to the culture and climate of each particular setting. The lot for the new Dutch embassy on the outskirts of Addis Ababa, the capital of Ethiopia, comprised 12 acres of eucalyptus woodland, with a gentle slope rolling down to the central valley. The preexisting historical villa was rebuilt and enlarged to provide the deputy ambassador's residence and three homes for chancery staff, as well as offices and the main public entrance. This building, situated in the middle of the lot and surrounded by eucalyptus trees, consists of a longitudinal volume that seems to have been excavated out of the rock, just as churches were traditionally constructed in Ethiopia. This effect was achieved through the imposing appearance of the volume (made up of a single rectangular piece), its proportion of solid mass with respect to hollow areas, and the meticulous construction process—not to mention the selection of materials. All the exterior cladding consists of rough concrete—which emphasizes the imprinted texture of its ornamentation—while its reddish color accurately mimics that of the land around it.

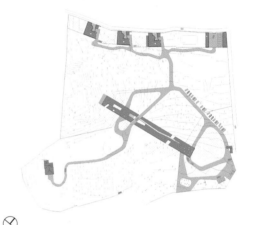

Site Plan

Client
Dutch Foreign Ministry

Type of Project
Embassy, chancery, and residences

Location
Addis Ababa, Ethiopia

Total Surface Area
35,521 square feet (3,300 m²)

Completion Date
2005

Photos ©
Christian Richters

Addis Ababa, Ethiopia

Dutch Embassy

Dick van Gameren, Bjarne Mastenbroek

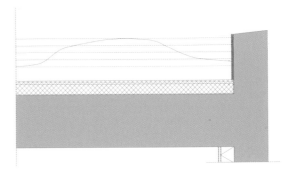

Detail, Section of the Roof

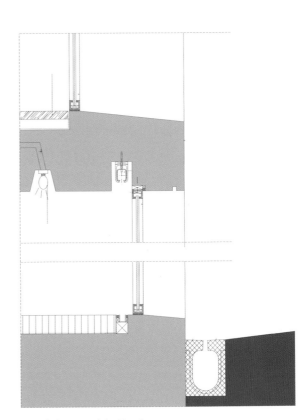

Detail, Section of the Façade

The natural landscape seems to penetrate the building in the middle section, thanks to the large opening that divides the volume in two. This device not only serves to separate the residential area from the offices but also emphasizes the building's role as a point of access. The road running through the lot passes underneath the volume, thus creating a sheltered entrance for visitors and residents alike. While the north and south elevations consist of a single continuous surface, the east and west elevations resemble carved and modeled stone. The roof, first seen in the section of the road running alongside the top part of the building, was conceived as a shallow artificial pool that recalls the plains of the Netherlands in the midst of the rugged landscape of Ethiopia.

Plan of the Roof

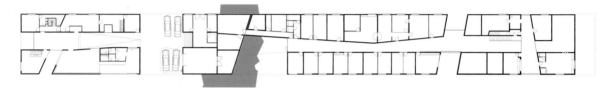

Second Floor

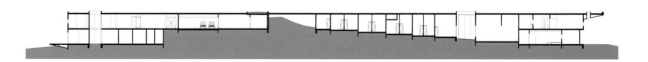

Gound Floor

Longitudinal Section

The embassy's interior composition is simple, with offices on both sides of a central corridor that follows the slope of the terrain. The entrance is situated at the end of the corridor, in the lowest part, where the height that has been gained made it possible to add an intermediate level, containing the ambassador's office (reached via the same staircase that leads to the roof). The residential area, on the other side of the volume, is spread over two stories, with the formal and social rooms on the upper level and the private quarters on the lower floor (where the lay of the land allows both housing units to enjoy direct access to the garden).

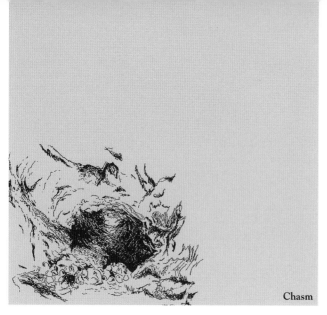

Chasm

Braga Municipal Stadium is situated within the Dume Sports Park, on the northern edge of Monte Castro. This park location was chosen to avoid the need to build a retention wall on the slopes of the valley, for the scale of such an intervention would have occasioned an excessive impact on the natural surroundings. It was therefore decided to place the stadium farther to the west and support it with the mountainsides, along the lines of a Roman amphitheater excavated out of the land. This option not only provided a solution to problems concerning the landscape and environment, it also responded to a highly personal vision of soccer as spectacle. Nowadays, this sport has become mass entertainment, just like the movies, theater, and television—fields that all served as inspiration for the creation of this scenic architecture. These considerations also led to the decision to build just two longitudinal banks of bleachers, facing each other, and to leave the sides open to the mountain at one end and the city at the other. The roof was originally drawn as a large canopy, similar to that of the Portuguese pavilion designed by Alvaro Siza for the Lisbon Expo. However, the conditions of the site and technical considerations eventually prompted the architect to turn for inspiration to the Incan hanging bridges in Peru, which span huge distances across the steep valleys of the Andes.

Site Plan

Client
Cámara Municipal de Braga

Type of Project
Sports facility

Location
Braga, Portugal

Capacity
33,000 spectators

Completion Date
2003

Photos ©
Christian Richters

Braga Municipal Stadium

Souto Moura Architects

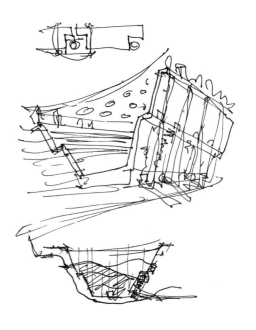

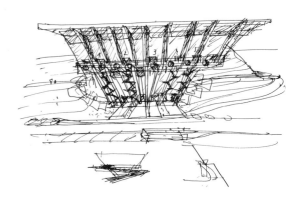

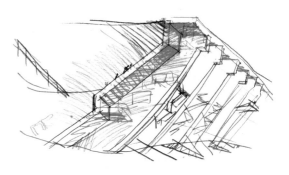

Preliminary Sketches

The two themes of voids and emptied spaces recur throughout the design of this project. The volume functions as a vessel, both concave and convex, that is surrounded and broken on successive occasions, creating an ambiguous relationship with the terrain. The stadium is surrounded by voids—in front, below, behind, and on the sides—and by emptied spaces compressed between the concave surface of the bleachers and the convex one of the rock (the two never touch). The 131-foot (40-m) construction comprises two facing rectangular planes, which are sloped at the same angle to form the bleachers. This strategy allows the structure to become a reference for any future development of this expanding area north of the city, while also guaranteeing its transparency and continuity.

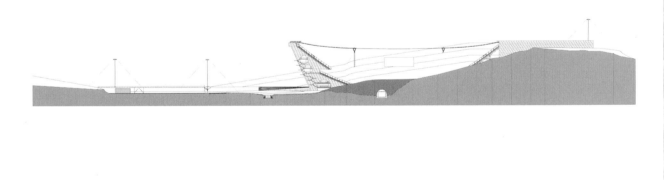

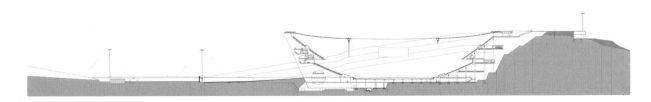

Longitudinal Sections

The main public area is reached via an esplanade (delimited by a plantation of birch trees) that serves as a parking lot. From this large square, the visitor goes up a slight slope, diagonal to the stadium, that offers a view of its concave form. Further on, this foreshortening gives way to a frontal view, which makes it possible to appreciate the monumentality of the concrete, with its systematic and modern order. Since the structure is embedded in the rock and is inaccessible on its short, open ends, spectators are obliged to enter from the sides before climbing to the top of the bleachers, where the excavated rock wall can be seen. This path involves the use of pillars, stairs, elevators, and service hubs, like a journey through a labyrinthine cavern.

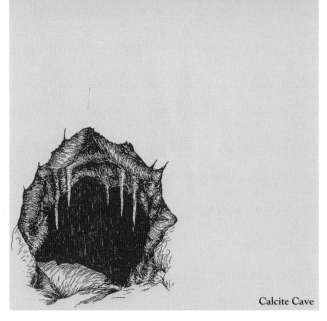

Calcite Cave

The Gotthard Visitors' Center in Pollegio, southern Switzerland, is the first of two buildings that will form the two entrances to the Gotthard train tunnel. These two buildings are intended to be emblematic of the complexity and significance of infrastructural architecture in the twenty-first century. The fleeting image of the tunnel snatched by a traveler in the region cannot do justice to the true scope of such an achievement, so the visitors' center was added precisely to explain the difficulties of the construction and its importance for the future. In fact, the 35-mile (57-km) tunnel through the middle of a mountain represented an authentic technological and imaginative challenge, and the center will serve to reveal the marvels involved in a project of this kind. In an era when society has managed to reduce distances by eliminating materiality, a tunnel is a specific materialization of distance. These days, we can talk to somebody on the other side of a mountain just by dialing a number on a cell phone, but this project will take over twelve years of arduous labor to enable physical contact to be made between these two points. These small buildings on either side of the mountain will stand as a celebration of the victory over the symbolic and mythical distance.

Site Plan

Client
Administration of Pollegio, Ticino

Type of Project
Tourist facility

Location
Pollegio, Switzerland

Total Surface Area
19,375 square feet (1,800 m²)

Completion Date
2003

Photos ©
Yves André

Gotthard Visitors' Center

bauzeit architekten

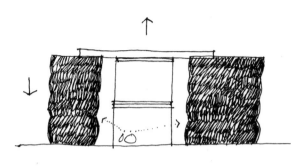

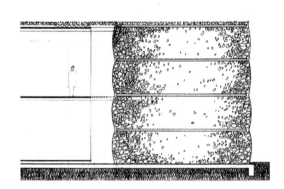

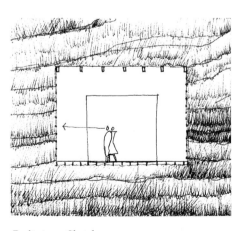

Preliminary Sketches

The buildings, made with material extracted from the entrails of the mountain, will face each other, as a symbol of the human urge to communicate more quickly and easily. Rather than a mere exhibition space, the buildings offer visitors an experience revolving around materiality, emptying, and distance. In this respect, the Gotthard Visitors' Center is a transposition of material into experience and not just a display of material. Visitors perceive not only the materiality of distance but also actually become involved in the excavation of the tunnel, by being able to feel its mass and the forces at work in the emptying of this space. The very walls that make up the building express these phenomena as they are formed by millions of stones extracted from the mountain.

The artificial topography proposed by this project gently leads the visitor from the exterior of the building to the lobbies and inside rooms, on a path running through a series of multi-purpose spaces.

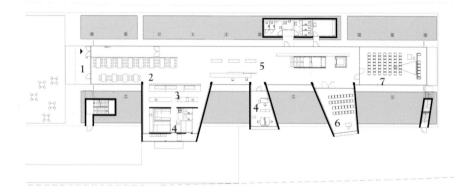

Ground Floor

1- Entrance
2- Reading Area
3- Cloakroom
4- Offices
5- Permanent Exhibition
6- Conference Room
7- Projection Room

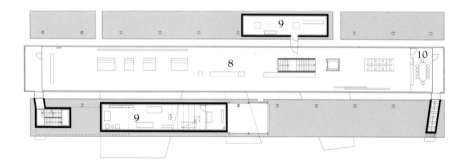

Second Floor

8- Temporary Exhibition
9- Storage Area
10- Meeting Room

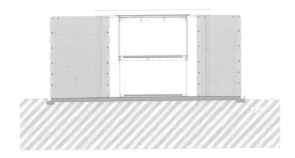

Cross Section

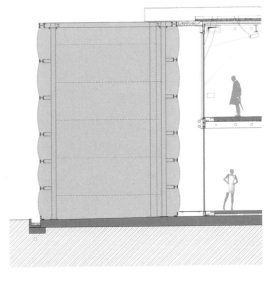

Construction Detail

To construct the perimeter walls, a selection had to be made from the rocks with a diameter of 4 to 6 inches (100 to 150 mm) extracted from the mountain, to fill the large steel baskets that serve as the building's structural support. The main rooms in the center are spread over two levels suspended from a steel structure fixed to the baskets of rock. The glass walls, anchored to this metal structure, create an independent sensorial and visual unity, while helping to control the temperature inside the building. The service areas, such as the restrooms and storage spaces, are situated in reinforced-concrete boxes, hidden inside the baskets of rock. Due to the impact of the space and the handling of such strongly contrasting materials, the main hall is defined by the contrast between materiality and immateriality.

Cave Section

"God created Lusatia, but the Devil put coal underneath it" is a popular saying among the inhabitants of this historical region, now part of the state of Saxony in Germany. Black coal has been both a curse and a blessing for the area, which lived for decades from mining but paid a very high price: the natural landscape—along with over 130 towns—has been totally or partially swept away by excavations associated with mining. This archive, which consists of a multimedia documentation center, surveys the fortunes of thousands of people affected by this process, as well as honoring the memory of vanished places and illustrating rehousing policies, both past and present. The morphological characteristics of the region's topography—underlaid at a depth of only a few yards by the precious mineral—and its mining techniques were the conceptual references used by the architects to draw up this project. The surface layer that was eliminated to create the quarries was conceived as a carpet wrapped around itself to create the volume and the interior of the documentation center. It is an intelligent carpet incorporating multimedia techniques, offering the visitor extensive information about the landscape that existed in this region until just a few decades ago.

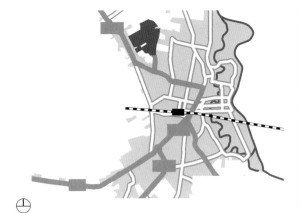

Site Plan

Client
Municipality of Forst and Vattenfall

Type of Project
Cultural facility

Location
Lusatia, Germany

Total Surface Area
538 square feet (50 m^2)

Completion Date
2005

Photos ©
Stefan Meyer

Archive of Vanished Places

Peanutz Architekten

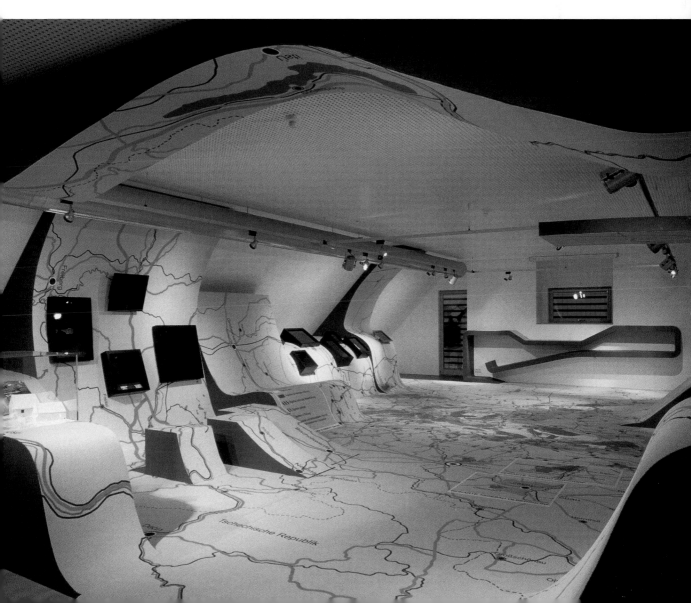

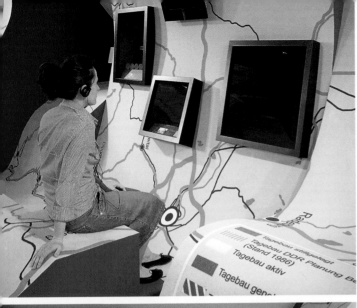

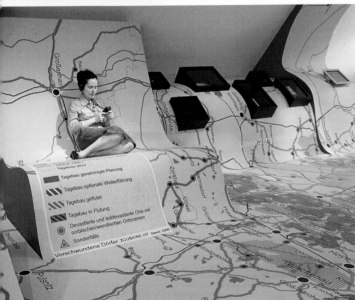

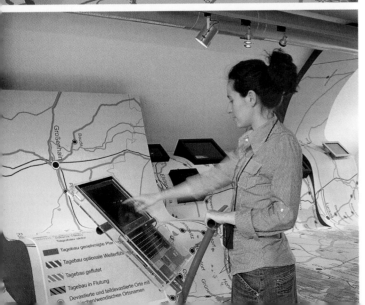

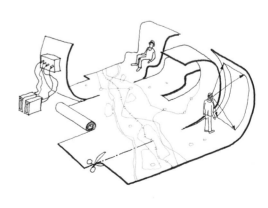

Conceptual Diagrams

A map of Lusatia is printed on the carpet lining the space, along with certain geographical and social data. The visitor can use mobile scanners to explore the map, choose a site, and find information about it. When the scanner pauses over a vanished town, the visitor can access data, such as images of its church, film of a popular festival, an interview, a map of the town, the number of inhabitants, or the history of the spot. Every scanner is a computer terminal that receives data from a central server, which also updates information about the changing face of this distinctive landscape.

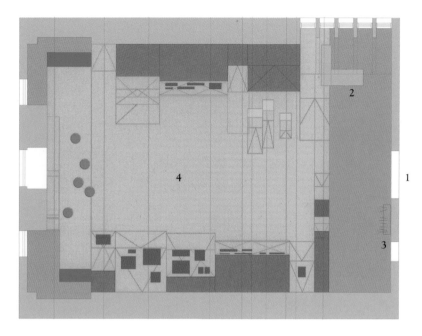

General Ground Plan

1- Entrance
2- Reception
3- Cloakroom
4- Exhibition Gallery

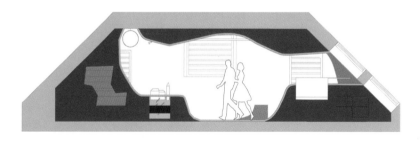

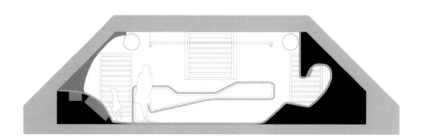

Cross Sections

The sinuous forms of the plywood panels that define the interior create an "unending" effect as the space's edges are left undetermined, thereby taking full advantage of the archive's limited dimensions.

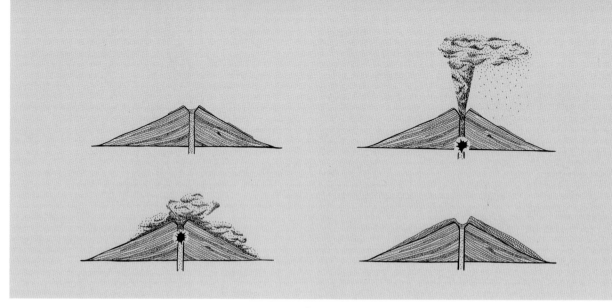

Eruption

Volcanoes

Beyond our conception of minerals as inert, stable material—a symbol of immutability—the crystals, rocks, and other forms that they generate are in a continuous process of transformation, creation, and destruction. As they are living organisms, all forms in the mineral world experience a birth or appearance, a process of growth, modification, and displacement, and then a disappearance, be it erosion, evaporation, reincorporation into magmatic material, etc. What makes minerals seem inert to us is the time scale in which these phenomena occur. The millions of years taken to form a mountain or the subtle movements of the tectonic plates are imperceptible to human eyes.

With this in mind, speaking of architectural projects that draw on the concept of the transformation of mineral ma-terial may seem somewhat contrived, but some transforma-tions that are immediate or operate on a human time scale can help us to understand the processes underlying the for-mation of the earth and so prove immensely attractive. One of the most spectacular of such processes—as it can unfurl in a matter of months, weeks, hours, or even minutes—is the eruption of a volcano, with its eye-catching ejection of mineral material. This phenomenon has always aroused enormous interest in humans, not only because of the fear instilled by its cruel, destructive power, but also as a result of its capacity to fashion new mineral landscapes. Over the course of human history, the unpredictability of volcanoes' activity and the intermittence of their eruptions has been evidenced by the engulfing of countless human settle-

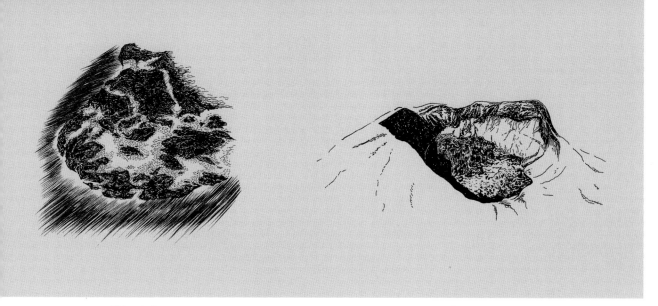

Volcanic Lava   Crater

ments, turned into mass graves. The ruins of Pompeii, lying at the feet of Vesuvius, represent one of the most chilling examples of the destructive capacity of the molten rock that lurks inside the earth when it comes to the surface and hardens. On a visit to Pompeii, Sir Walter Scott repeatedly called it the "City of Death," and indeed innumerable people were entombed in the onrush of ashes and lava on that August morning of 79 A.D., unchecked by any buildings. As in the case of Pompeii, volcanic eruptions, like other phenomena that reflect activity inside the earth, almost always give rise to so-called natural disasters. Regardless of whether they are interpreted as expressions of the gods' anger or of the earth's thermal energy, they reveal—more than any other circumstances—the fragile aspects of architecture.

Buildings' inability to provide a refuge often makes them an accomplice in the tragedy and gives human beings a brutal lesson in humility.

It is not uncommon to find features in contemporary buildings set in volcanic areas that invite reflection about the futility of human construction in the face of nature's aggression. The use of solidified lava is an ideal means to this end, as it provides a showcase for this stony liquid, capable of implacably overwhelming everything in its path. Furthermore, the incorporation of amorphous volcanic material into a building establishes contrasts with enormous expressive power, in both formal and chromatic terms.

Volcanic Lava

The exceptional location of this conference center was of prime importance in the initial approach to the project. The volcanic landscape of Tenerife (one of the Canary Islands) and the presence of the sea in the distance were the two determining factors the architects took into account to create a reference point in an area dominated by anonymous buildings. The building is situated on high ground that offers panoramic views of the coast and the island of La Gomera. The idea was to produce an expressive object of power and formal arrogance that would nevertheless be integrated into the landscape when seen from a distance. The composition is based on thirteen geometric pieces that emerge from the ground and contain the program's various complementary services: offices, restrooms, café, etc. These blocks rise to create a blurred line of movement through the flow of the roof, imagined as a sinuous liquid that bounds space in all directions. This surface undulates and separates, just like magma, to create cracks for light and ventilation. It is broken and multiplied, thereby intensifying the sensation of lightness and movement. From a functional viewpoint, the roof's undulations and fluctuations fulfill the technical requirements for the acoustics, which were calculated and adjusted after numerous studies. The space defined between the rocks emerging from the ground contains the lobby areas and conference halls, as well as other multipurpose spaces.

Site Plan

Client
Canarias Congress Bureau Tenerife Sur

Type of Project
Conference center

Location
Costa Adeje, Tenerife, Spain

Total Surface Area
220,660 square feet (20,500 m²)

Completion Date
2005

Photos ©
Torben Eskerod

Magma Conference Center

AMP Arquitectos

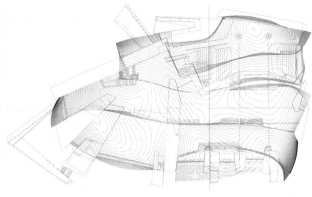

Topography of the Roof

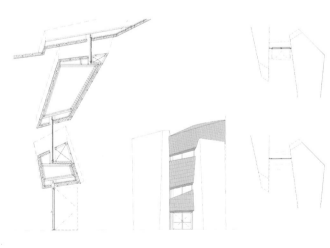

Façade Details

The ground-floor conference hall, with a capacity of 2,500 people, can be subdivided into nine smaller halls with a seating capacity of 300 each. The upper story contains the lecture room, which can accommodate 20 to 200 people after interior division. This transformation is performed by means of soundproofed panels set within the reinforced-concrete perimeter modules. The choice of materials reflects the underlying intention to integrate the building into the landscape—so, for example, the concrete was made with a type of local sand, while the roof features vegetal-fiber panels, both inside and outside, with a tinted finish that assimilates the colors of its surroundings.

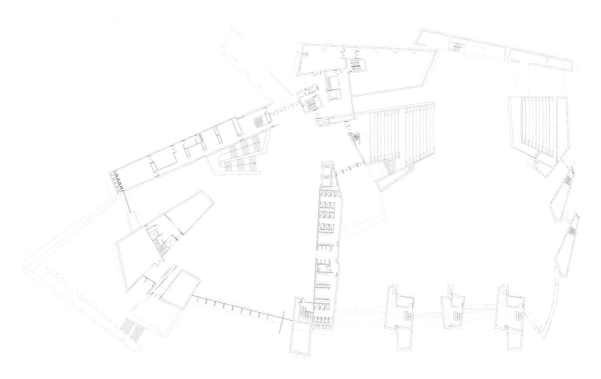

General Ground Plan

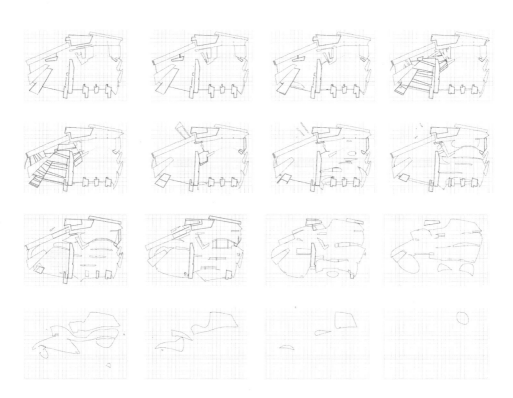

Evolution of the Plan

Over the course of its construction, as a result of the modifications made to the program, this building functioned like a changing organism. This made it possible to convert a simple conference center into a building capable of hosting an extremely wide range of cultural events, thereby endowing the southern part of Tenerife with a cultural infrastructure that was hitherto lacking. Several experts, particularly from the fields of sound and acoustics, made crucial contributions to the building's technical definition. Numerous working models—made with building materials and modified on a daily basis—helped determine the inner structure of the roof and achieve optimal acoustics. The fruit of this constantly evolving process can be seen in the great expressiveness of the building, which blends with the landscape perfectly.

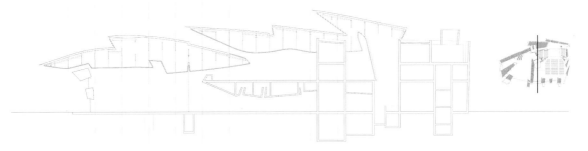

Cross Section

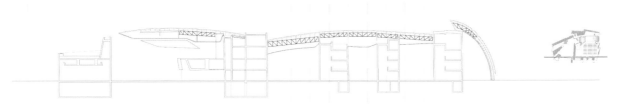

Longitudinal Section

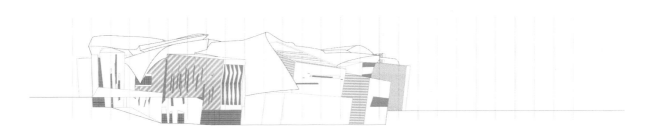

West Elevation

South Elevation

The interior of the conference center is distinguished by the variety of forms and finishes that have been extracted from the basic construction material—concrete—from the huge, rough beams to the small details on several interior walls.

Eruption

The César Manrique Foundation administers the abundant legacy of the brilliant artist from the Canary Isles who gives it its name. Born in 1919 in Arrecife, the capital of the island of Lanzarote, Manrique studied architecture for two years before devoting himself to painting and sculpture, becoming a key figure on the island's artistic scene in the 1970s and 1980s. The value of his work was primarily due to the understanding, respect, and creativity it displayed toward the island's natural settings, as seen in outdoor installations like the Volcanic Water Tubes, the River Observation Point, and the Cactus Garden. Manrique's own house, called El Taro de Tahíche, was built in 1968 and turned into the headquarters of his foundation in 1992. A recent project enlarged and refurbished the premises to adapt the building to its new function as a museum and art gallery for work by both Manrique and other artists. The program also had to provide studio spaces for artists working at the foundation for limited periods of time. The major challenge—apart from the dialogue with the existing building—consisted of fitting into the lunar landscape created by relatively fresh lava, originating from eruptions in the eighteenth century, with volcanic mountains as the backdrop and the ocean visible in the distance. The building emerges as a subtle structure, a horizontal line framing the lava landscape, with most of the facility underground.

Site Plan

Client
César Manrique Foundation

Type of Project
Museum

Location
Lanzarote, Spain

Total Surface Area
5,113 square feet (475 m²)

Completion Date
2004

Photos ©
Roland Halbe

César Manrique Foundation

Palerm + Tabares de Nava Arquitectos

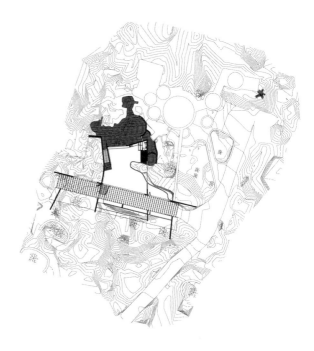

Ground Floor

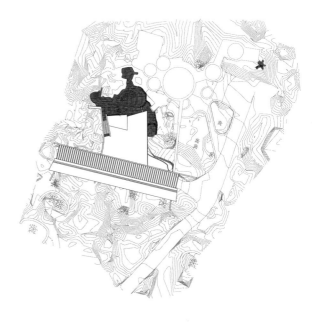

Plan of the Roofs

The lava covering the land was the basic element of the project's composition, and the island's natural stone was the raw material for its construction. Most of the reinforced-concrete structure supporting the building was clad with volcanic stone, to allow the interior of the space to be completely integrated into the outdoor topography. This integration is emphasized by the enormous windows stretching from floor to ceiling and the angular concrete roofs, which also serve as terraces and observation platforms. In this project, the architects used an idiom based on the esthetic of the Modern movement, and deliberately distanced themselves from the discreet, enclosed colonial architecture of the foundation's original building just a few meters away.

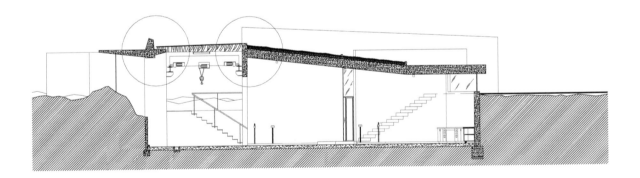

Construction Section

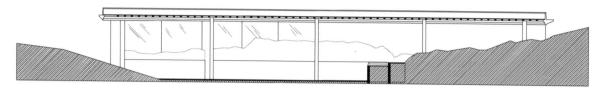

Longitudinal Section

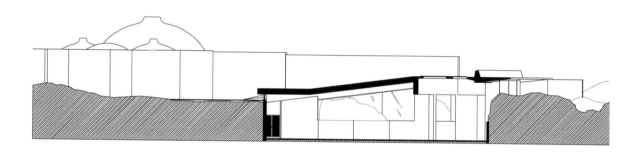

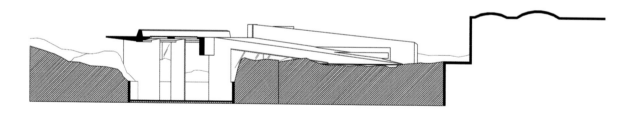

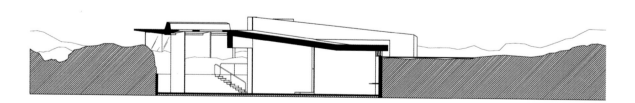

Cross Sections

The geometric purity that defines the building from the outside is also evident in the interior, thereby emphasizing still further the striking lava landscape that surrounds—and sometimes invades—the building.

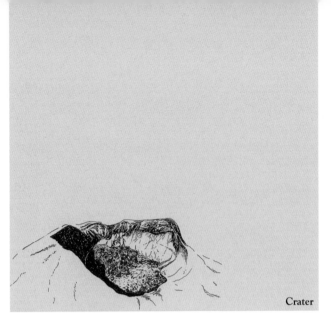

Crater

The urban landscape of Santa Cruz de Tenerife in the Canary Islands displays a combination of striking features—the permanent view of the sea, the uneven lay of the land, the uncontrolled property development, and the imposing presence of the Teide, an inactive volcano that is the highest peak in Spain and determines the island's physiognomy. The architects' basic premises for their proposal for this stadium were integration into the surrounding urban fabric; an optimal north-northeast placement for the athletics stadium; a unified, monumental sense of scale; and the importance of spectator's sightlines. Taking as their starting point the topography of the site, particularly the difference in the level from one end to the other, they came up with bleachers that take advantage of part of the natural slope, complemented by an embankment made with soil excavated from the ground. The building takes its place as a large entrance square containing the covered installations. On a metropolitan scale, the project stands as more than just a building, but rather as a large crater opened up in the middle of the urban fabric. This aspect considerably reduces the visual impact of the infrastructure and integrates the intervention into the natural landscape that dominates the island.

Site Plan

Client
Cabildo de Tenerife, Santa Cruz de Tenerife City Council

Type of Project
Sports facility

Location
Santa Cruz de Tenerife, Spain

Total Surface Area
384,379 square feet (35,710 m²)

Completion Date
2007

Photos ©
Hisao Suzuki

Santa Cruz de Tenerife, Spain

Athletics Stadium

AMP Arquitectos·

Preliminary Sketches

The construction system, based on the repetition of concrete screens, reduced the cost of a project with a highly
significant structural component. The athletic track was
designed according to international requirements and is
complemented by training areas around the edges. The
inner area was conceived as a flexible space that can also
be used for gymnastics. The complex also includes a residential area to accommodate athletes or officials from the
center; this is set in the southeast part of the building, to
take full advantage of the views and natural light. The
bleachers were originally planned to hold 4,000 spectators,
but the remains of the natural slope subsequently made it
possible to enlarge them to accommodate 6,000 people.

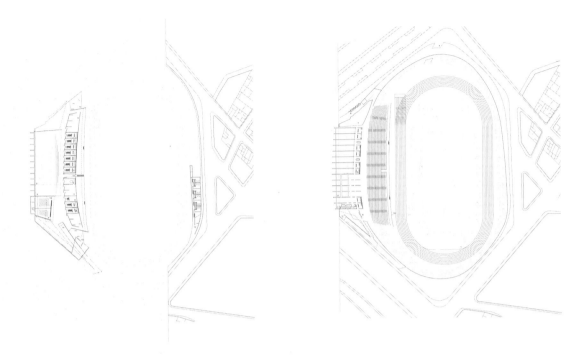

Ground Floor

Plan of the Bleachers

Longitudinal Section

Cross Section

The most important feature of the stadium, in both formal and structural terms, consists of the concrete screens in the form of a V that define the building's volumes and make it possible to keep the use of concrete to the minimum.

Monolith

Monolith

The Monolith

Of the three states of material—liquid, gas, and solid—only the latter displays strong, fixed bonds between its molecules. Solid bodies have the ability to support pressure without any apparent deformation; they are therefore generally aggregates that are stiff, hard, and resistant. While water is liquid and air is gaseous, the mineral element unequivocally represents "solidity" on our planet. Architecture, seen by Le Corbusier as an interplay of volumes under light, inevitably turns its gaze to the standard-bearer for solidity—stone—with all its mineral components and the landscapes they give rise to. The analogy between an isolated piece of architecture and the monolith as a geological structure, represented by a single massive rock, has long been established. However, rather than referring to monolithic architecture—

impossible by definition, except in the case of monuments, as all buildings require space in order to be occupied—this chapter will explore the idea of the monolith as a metaphor.

Many buildings that convey an impression of solidity do not necessarily have the material properties of stone, or of a block or monolith, but try to act as if they do, by imitating the language of stone as a strategy of representation. The search for primary forms in architecture often springs from the need to convey sensations such as impregnability, solidity, hardness, solemnity, or weightiness. It is not unusual to find buildings specifically designed to protect their interior—bunkers or banks—in which extreme formal economy and simplicity

| Menhir | Dolmen |

make them look unassailable. In other cases, buildings that disguise their internal complexity behind a compact packaging can achieve a highly individualized expression akin to monumentality. Through their formal language, they can take on a gravitas that seems to absorb any excesses of neighboring buildings.

The search for formal economy usually arises from a need for financial economy. "The more symmetrical, regular, and simple a building, the less expensive it will be" (J. N. Louis Durand, *Précis des Leçons d'Architecture*, 1801–3). While the construction of monolithic buildings is cheaper because of the simplicity derived from the repetition of modular solu-tions or the use of prefabricated materials, the design process is also simplified. The fact that design techniques based on computer programs have emerged at the same time as a prolif-eration of monolithic architecture is no accident. Computers spurn ornamented forms and uneven volumes, while seeking continuous surfaces with regular patterns.

Finally, the choice of primitive geometric forms often reflects an attempt to flee from excessive ornamentation in architec-ture. Adolf Loos, in his crusade against ornament, conceived buildings with no attributes, closer to an industrial product than traditional Viennese architecture. He used the materials themselves to endow his buildings with ornamental value.

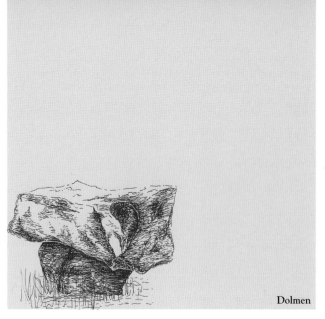

Dolmen

Back in 1996, when the architect of this project was invited to participate in a select competition, he started assessing and tackling the various factors determining the project, which involved creating bank offices in a region that had been in Communist hands before the fall of the Berlin Wall. The area bore the marks of Central European culture, as well as the vestiges of the adventure of the Modern movement—particularly the tensions between rigor, repetition, technique, and expressive urges. Apart from these cultural considerations, the lot for the building was lacking in any great conceptual or compositional impact. It is set in the middle of the Park der Opfer des Faschismus (Park for the Victims of Fascism), a natural wooded area that has been absorbed into Chemnitz's urban fabric with barely any alteration. The park is notable for its centuries-old trees and two reminders of European military history: a buried French patrol, killed during the Napoleonic wars, and a neglected monument to the dead of World War II. Adolf Loos defended tombs as the maximum expression of architecture, and these graves represent signifying tokens, set against the natural reference of the huge trees. The nearby Museum of Paleontology—a reflection of the alchemical transformation that turns living matter into inert stone—ended up guiding the design approach to this project. The building was conceived as a stony fossil that offers glimpses of a different organic consistency from the distant past.

Site Plan

Client
Deutsche Bundesbank

Type of Project
Bank offices

Location
Chemnitz, Germany

Total Surface Area
102,257 square feet (9,500 m²)

Completion Date
2004

Photos ©
Jan Bitter / Bitter Fotografie

New Deutsche Bundesbank Offices

MAP Architects / Josep Lluís Mateo

Façade Detail

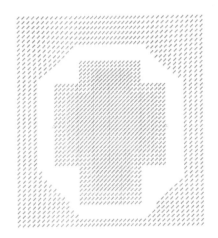

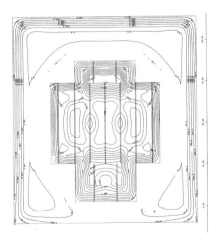

Structural Diagrams

The translucent façade is fundamental to the materialization of the concept underlying the project. This is the idea of a petrified tree—sunk in and anchored to the ground—that displays varying patterns of the sky, while the inorganic hardness of the stone contrasts with the solidified vegetal structure. Onyx and alabaster immediately sprang to mind as ideal options for the cladding. The enclosures are arranged on cables, brought to a state of tension by springs in their upper sections. The tension applied to the cable varies according to the weather conditions, which are monitored by computer. This makes it possible for the vertical uprights to be very thin, as they are in a permanent state of traction. The enclosing panels are laminated with several layers of glass, alternating with sheets of stone. The latter was chosen for its capacity to react to the outdoor conditions with markings that can appear and disappear, thereby endowing this inert material with organic qualities.

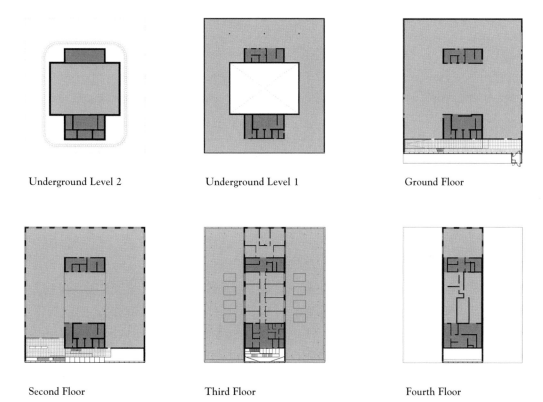

Underground Level 2   Underground Level 1   Ground Floor

Second Floor   Third Floor   Fourth Floor

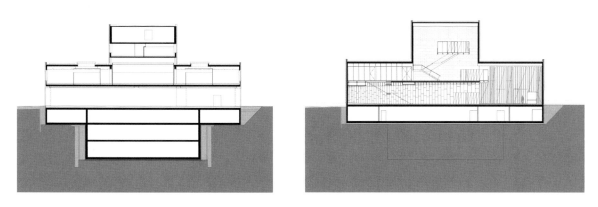

Longitudinal sections

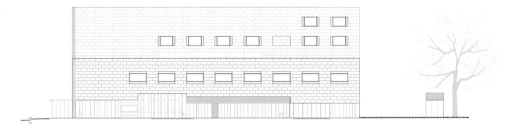

South Elevation

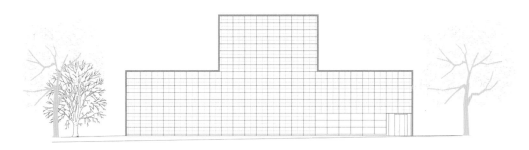

West Elevation

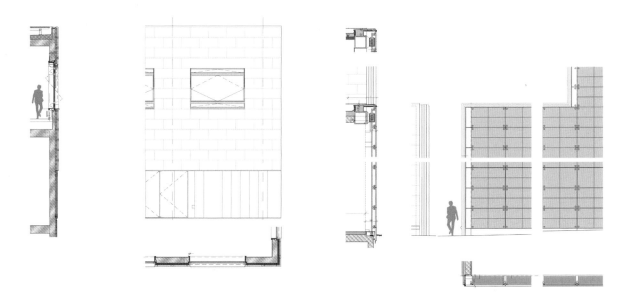

Detail of the South Façade   Detail of the West Façade

The laminar composite created by the building's cladding was tested in a laboratory to ensure that it could resist harsh weather conditions and fulfill stringent security requirements. The panels are joined to the structure and connected to each other by frames, along the lines of standardized construction for curtain walls. The materials chosen for the frames and outdoor elements emphasized the archaic nature of the building. The corners are made of a single carved stone, the base of slightly rougher stone, and the windows of bronze and wood. The interior of the entrance lobby—the most monumental and public part of the building—develops the metaphor of the fossil through the addition of stones and pieces of trees.

Monolith

The bunker has become a familiar feature of the Dutch land-scape, having emerged in the early twentieth century for military purposes and as protection against flooding. The first structures of this kind in the Vreeswijk valley date back to 1936; they served to reinforce nineteenth-century defensive constructions put up along the waterline. This region's landscape is distinguished by a 53-mile (85-km) loop comprising military installations, as well as a complex damming system that enables the area to be flooded in the case of attack. Bunkers have therefore played a major his-torical role and become a typical part of the classic polder land-scape of the Netherlands. Over time, bunkers lost their defensive function and so they have been given over to other uses, as parts of schools, sports facilities, or commercial premises. This project, with a simple program involving a leisure pavilion for an office complex, was approached as a contemporary interpretation of the type of architecture characteristic of the region. The solidity aris-ing from the continuous surface unbroken by openings contrasts with the lightness of the angular geometry and the placement of part of the building as a projection onto the land.

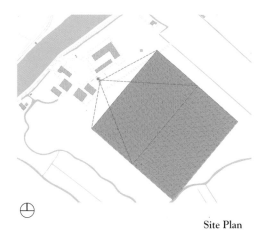

Site Plan

Client
Private

Type of Project
Leisure pavilion

Location
Vreeswijk, Netherlands

Total Surface Area
861 square feet (80 m²)

Completion Date
2005

Photos ©
Christian Richters

Tea House Bunker

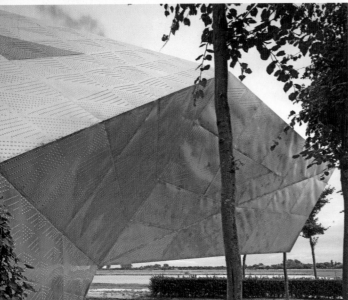

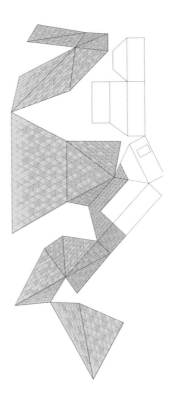

Flattened View of the Façades

Exploded Axonometry

The project consists of an enlargement of an old bunker that had already been used as a spillover area from a near-by office building. The structure in the form of a three-dimensional curved metal support and the stainless-steel cladding serve to both cover and extend the original bunker, which had previously contained service and storage areas. The installation of the building's exterior cladding required all the façades to be stretched out geometrically, with a single triangular module of cladding as its starting point. The repetition of this module and the folding of the building's general perimeter, reminiscent of origami, resolve the pavilion's complex geometry.

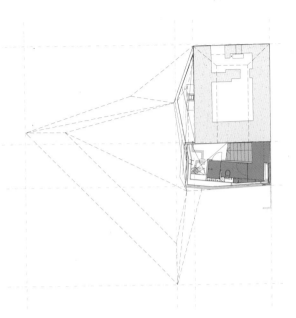

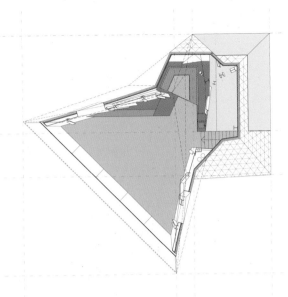

Ground Floor

Second Floor

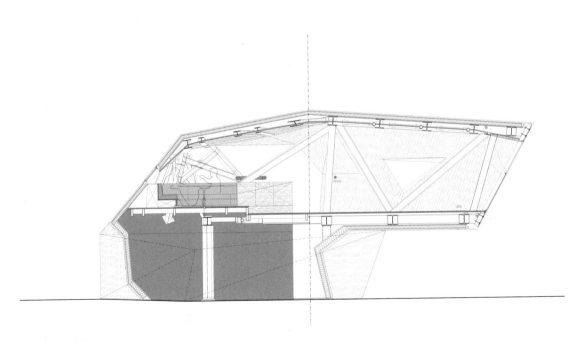

Longitudinal Section

The building's monolithic appearance is due not only to its distinctive volumes, which summon up images of carved stone, but also to the technical achievement of a continuous, edged cladding that runs around the entire structure.

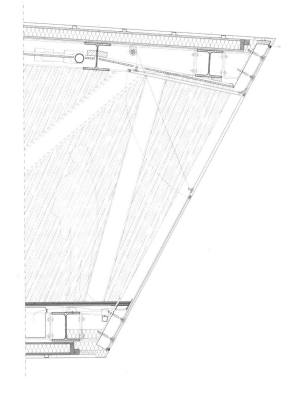

Façade Detail

The interior space, with no partitions or installations, can be adapted to diverse activities. It can serve as a meeting room, a venue for parties, or an area for taking time out during the work day. The various fissures created by the stainless-steel strips culminate in a large window—the only one in the building—that opens right up to become a big balcony with a view over the adjoining polo fields. This continuous glass window emphasizes the building's technological aspects—as it is similar to the structure of a car—as well as its monolithic character.

Monolith

The small town of Hinzert is surrounded by an idyllic, typically German landscape with rolling mountains and orderly fields. Nothing betrays the fact that, between 1939 and 1945, this was the site of a special concentration camp for political prisoners from over twenty countries. The project, whose design resulted from an open competition for ideas for the region's documentation center and museum, tries to delve into the political and territorial transformations that the area has undergone. The wide-ranging program for the complex included archives, a research bookshop, lecture rooms, and exhibition spaces. The architects, internationally acclaimed for their synagogue in Dresden, demonstrated once again their desire to investigate the relationship between materials and their potential conceptual qualities. This building's unconventional design is based on both rational development strategies and pure intuition. It consists of a volume 141 feet (43 m) long, set on the top of a gently sloping hill, and its structure, form, and exterior finish give it an enigmatic, sculptural quality in the middle of the landscape. The single shell formed by the façades and roof comprises almost 3,000 different steel plates ½-inch (12 mm) thick, presoldered to create 12 larger elements that were subsequently assembled in situ.

Site Plan

Client
Land Rheinland-Pfalz, LBB Trier, Central Office of Public Works

Type of Project
Documentation center and museum

Location
Hinzert, Germany

Total Surface Area
9,182 square feet (853 m²)

Completion Date
2005

Photos ©
Norbert Miguletz

Hinzert Documentation Center and Museum

Wandel Hoefer Lorch + Hirsch

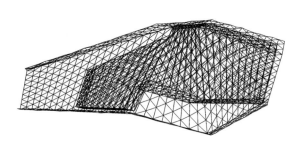

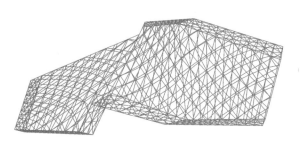

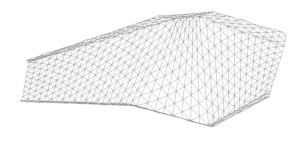

Three-Dimensional Digital Models

The angles between the various metallic plates were calculated by means of three-dimensional digital models in order to guarantee that the elements had a suitable structural weight and that the overall construction formed one rigid piece. The reddish-brown cladding shrouds an elongated space containing galleries and lecture rooms, a bookshop, an archive, and several offices. The design process unfurled outward from the interior area, with various units grouped around the central exhibition space, thereby pushing the limits of the volume toward the exterior landscape. Like a sealed surround protecting the historical material, the volume opens onto the valley at only one end, creating a nexus between the historical images and the view of today.

Despite the reiteration of the same geometry, there is a gap of up to 6 inches (15 cm) between the weathering steel wrapping the exterior and the birch ply panels cladding the interior, and this is filled with various layers of insulating material.

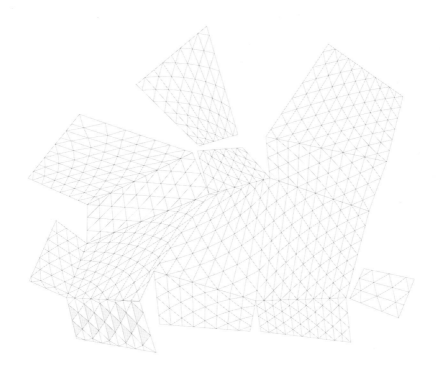

Flattened View of Façades

Flattened View of Interior

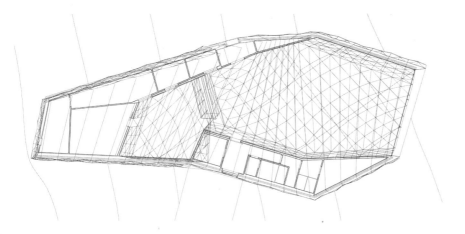

Ground Plan

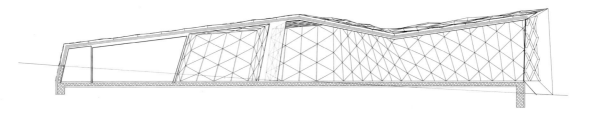

Longitudinal Section

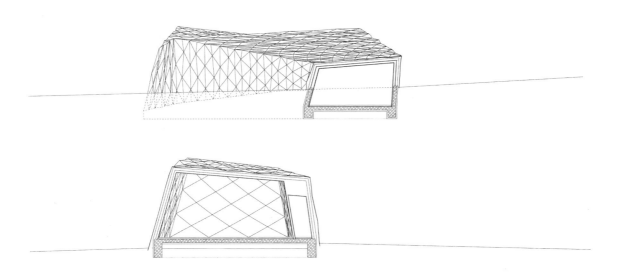

Cross Sections

The uniform spatial hierarchy that has been applied to all the spaces, and the interior design of the various spaces, emphasizes the idea that each section shares the same indoor space. The interior cladding consists of birch ply panels onto which photos and texts have been printed directly—the documents are not stuck onto the building but inserted right into it, like a contemporary reworking of a fresco. In order to achieve the optimal insulation between the exterior metal cladding and the wooden interior, specific prototypes were built for the project, including the openings, windows, doors, and triangular frames.

Monolith

This house was designed for a couple with two children who were interested in sharing their outdoor activities with the community. The intention was to create a setting where the children from the neighborhood could play and be supervised. In this respect, the location of the lot was crucial to the development of the project: it was situated at the far end of a group of isolated houses in a residential neighborhood in Heyri, South Korea. It occupied a key spot, at the end of the row of houses, on the border between the street and the back gardens. The public and the private coexist in a way not found in any other lot on the street. The project's strategy was based on the idea of breaking with the architectural uniformity in the neighborhood, and more particularly on the street, by creating a single solid piece that was also fragmented in its texture. The monolithic nature of this architectural object establishes a close relationship with the natural landscape, rather than emphasizing the architectural barrier formed by the row of neighboring houses. The volume, something between a rock and a building, thereby makes a visual statement by evoking the meeting point between the urbanized area and the natural world.

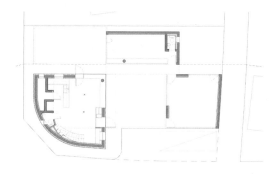

Site Plan

Client
Private

Type of Project
Family house

Location
Heyri, South Korea

Total Surface Area
1,206 square feet (112 m²)

Completion Date
2001

Photos ©
Yong-Kwan Kim

Pixel House

Slade Architecture, Mass Studies

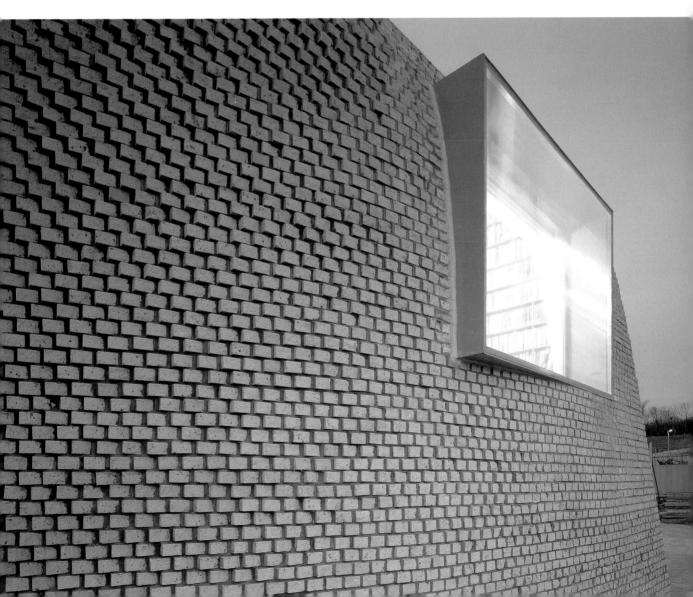

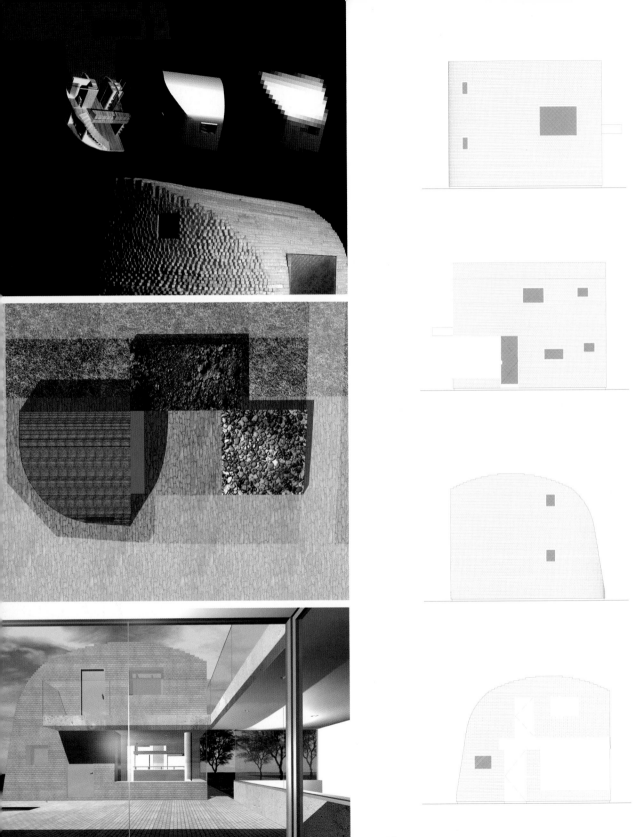

Elevations

The house's position, set back from the line of the façade on the street, emphasizes its monolithic character and establishes a tension between the buildings and the mountains around it—a tension also reflected in both the choice of materials and the building process. The use of typical solid brick kept the construction simple, while also allowing the volume to be broken down into discrete, minimal tectonic units. The brickwork also conveys a tangible impression of the building's scale, which seems to vary according to the distance from which it is seen. Just as a digital image is classified according to its quantity of pixels, the definition of this house is determined by its number of bricks. The result is a house with 9,675 pixels, where each pixel is the equivalent of one brick.

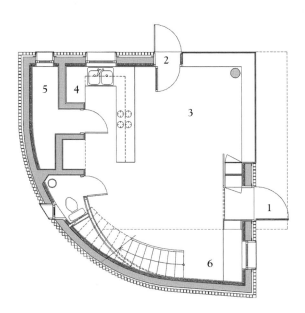

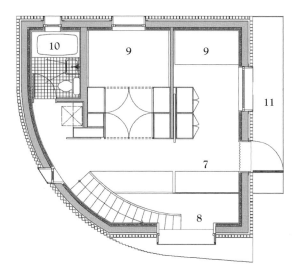

Ground Floor

1- Main Entrance
2- Entrance to the Garden
3- Lounge/Dining Room
4- Kitchen
5- Pantry
6- Study

Second Floor

7- Balcony Studio
8- Well to the Ground Floor
9- Bedroom
10- Bathroom
11- Balcony

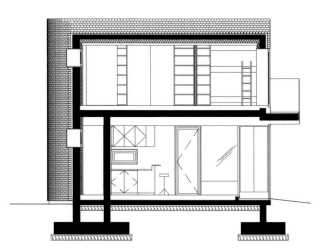

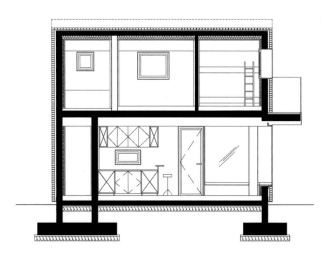

Longitudinal Sections

The interior of the house has been arranged as a continuous space that rises from the ground floor, containing the social area and kitchen, via a double-height space. The depth thus achieved on one side of the interior composition has been exploited to house the family's large collection of books. All the furniture elements, such as the shelves, work tables, doors, and benches, were conceived as an integral part of the architecture and serve to enhance the spatial relationships between the different spaces. So, the staircase leading to the upper floor, where the bedrooms are located, also serves as a lounge, library, or work studio.

Index of Architects

AMP Arquitectos
San Jose 2, Ático, Santa Cruz de Tenerife 38002, Spain
T: +34 922 245 149
F: +34 922 247 173
administracion@amparquitectos.com
www.amparquitectos.com

Antoine Predock
300 12th Street NW, Albuquerque, NM 87102, United States
T: +1 505 843 7390
F: +1 505 243 6254
studio@predock.com
www.predock.com

bauzeit architekten
Falkenstrasse 17, Biel 2502, Switzerland
T: +41 (0)32 344 6344
F: +41 (0)32 341 1175
info@bauzeit.com
www.bauzeit.com

Carsten Nicolai
c/o Galerie Eigen + Art
Auguststrasse 26, Berlín 10117, Germany
T: +49 30 2790 8498
F: +49 30 280 6616
noto@gmx.de
www.carstennicolai.de

Coop Himmelb(l)au
Spengergasse 37, Vienna 1050, Austria
T: +43 (0)1 546 60 334
F: +43 (0)1 546 60 600
ost@coop-himmelblau.at
www.coop-himmelblau.at

Daniel Libeskind
2 Rector Street, 19th floor, New York, NY 10006, United States
T: +1 212 497 9100
F: +1 212 285 2130
info@daniel-libeskind.com
www.daniel-libeskind.com

Dick van Gameren
Barentszplein 7, Amsterdam 1013, Netherlands
T: +31 (0)20 530 4850
F: +31 (0)20 530 4860
info@vangameren.com
www.vangameren.com

Dominique Perrault
26, rue Bruneseau, Paris 75013, France
T: +33 1 44 06 00 42
F: +33 1 44 06 00 01
dominique.perrault@perraultarchitecte.com
www.perraultarchitecte.com

Hertl.Architekten
Zwischenbrücken 4, Steyr 4400, Austria
T: +43 7252 46944
F: +43 7252 47363
steyr@hertl-architekten.com
www.hertl-architekten.com

MAP Architects/Josep Lluís Mateo
Teodoro Roviralta 39, Barcelona 08022, Spain
T: +34 932 186 358
F: +34 932 185 292
map@mateo-maparchitect.com
www.mateo-maparchitect.com

Mass Studies
Fuji Building. 4F
683-140 Hannam 2-dong Yongsan-gu, Seoul 140-892, Korea
T: +82 (0)2 790 6528/9
F: +82 (0)2 790 6438
office@massstudies.com
www.massstudies.com

Mueller Kneer Associates
18-20 Scrutton Street, London EC2 A 4EN, United Kingdom
T: +44 (0)20 7247 0993
F: +44 (0)20 7247 9935
info@muellerkneer.com
www.muellerkneer.com

Odile Decq Benoît Cornette
11, rue des Arquebusiers, Paris 75003, France
T: +33 1 42 71 27 41
F: +33 1 42 71 27 42
odbc@odbc-paris.com
www.odbc-paris.com

Palerm + Tabares de Nava Arquitectos
25 de Julio 48º, Santa Cruz de Tenerife 38004, Spain
T: +34 922 247 570
F: +34 922 282 765
paltab@paltab.com
www.paltab.com

Peanutz Architekten
Schlesische Strasse 12, Berlín 10997, Germany
T: +49 (0)30 44379033
F: +49 (0)30 44379010
post@peanutz-architekten.de
www.peanutz-architekten.de

Satoshi Okada Architects
16-12-302/303 Tomihisa, Shinjuku, Tokyo 162-0067, Japan
T: +81 3 3355 0646
F: +81 3 3355 0658
mail@okada-archi.com
www.okada-archi.com

Slade Architecture
150 Broadway 807, New York, NY 10038, United States
T: +1 212 677 6380
F: +1 212 677 6330
info@sladearch.com
www.sladearch.com

Souto Moura Arquitectos
Rua do Aleixo, 53-1ºA, Porto 4150-043, Portugal
T: +351 22 618 7547
F: +351 22 610 8092
souto.moura@mail.telepac.pt

Tadao Ando Architect & Associates
5-23 Toyosaki 2-Chome Kita-ku, Osaka, Japan
T: +81 6 6375 1148
F: +81 6 6374 6240

UNStudio
Stadhouderskade 113, Postbus 75381, Amsterdam 1070 AJ, Netherlands
T: +31 20 570 20 40
F: +31 20 570 20 41
info@unstudio.com
www.unstudio.com

Wandel Hoefer Lorch + Hirsch
Dolomitenweg 19, Saarbrücken 66119, Germany
T: +49 (0)681 92655 0
F: +49 (0)681 92655 95
info@wandel-hoefer-lorch.de
www. wandel-hoefer-lorch.de

Will Bruder Architects
2524 North 24th Street, Phoenix, AZ 85008, United States
T: +1 602 324 6022
F: +1 602 516 7022
studio@willbruder.com
www.willbruder.com

XTEN Architecture
201 S. Santa Fe Avenue, Suite 202, Los Angeles, CA 90012, United States
T: +1 213 625 7002
F: +1 213 625 7003
mail@xtenarchitecture.com
www.xtenarchitecture.com